FINDING A WAY

Frank Cremin

Diary of a walk from Lands End to John O'Groats

Printed and bound in Great Britain by Amazon

ISBN 9798843125905

BOLDMERE PRESS LIMITED

Boldmere, Royal Sutton Coldfield

B73 6NP

In memory of Frank Cremin

1948 – 2017

Missed every day

"If you really want to do something, you'll find a way.

If you don't you'll find an excuse

Day 1 Wednesday 26 April 2000 Lands End to Penzance

Wednesday, 26 April 2000 was a typical British spring morning; damp, overcast and with the threat of rain in the air. As my wife Carol and I waited at the bus stop, we took more than our usual passing interest in the weather, however. Rather than setting out for our jobs at offices after the Easter break, which had been our routine for many years, we were off to catch the train to Cornwall. We'd swapped our handbag and briefcase respectively for bulging rucksacks and were going to attempt something that we'd been talking about for years; walk from Lands End to John O'Groats.

I can't now remember exactly when we first thought of tackling what is, at around 900 miles, just about the longest walk that you can make in the British Isles. I suppose it started off like many pipedreams, something that we talked about on and off but perhaps never really thought we'd do. Gradually, however, "if we do it" became "when we do it". Perhaps the real catalyst was a TV play in which Joss Ackland's character fulfilled his dream of doing the walk, despite being diagnosed with, as I recall, cancer along the way. I really think that programme made us both determined to do it before we became too old and infirm.

There was never any doubt either that it would be both of us that made the attempt. We'd pretty much done everything together since what was an office romance began over 30 years earlier. We knew each other's strengths and weaknesses, rarely argued and, if we did, it was only ever over something trivial and soon over. We had also agreed that if one of us couldn't finish, he or she would act as support to the other, who would carry on.

Sponsorship was something that we'd discussed as a possibility more than once. Ian Botham had done the walk not long before we set out and raised over a million pound for his chosen cause. In general, however, we were not in favour. The walk was a personal challenge. Yes, we were determined to finish but for our own satisfaction. We'd been lucky in life and there was no real tragedy to motivate us. Moreover, if we couldn't finish then we wouldn't like to feel that we had let anyone down. Ultimately, however, and almost at the last minute, colleagues at Birmingham City Council, where I'd once worked and Carol still did, persuaded her to send some forms around the office. If we did finish, the Multiple Sclerosis Society would benefit to the extent of about £1,000.

Timing had also been an issue to be resolved. When would we go and how long would it take us? Spring or autumn were the obvious choices; we enjoyed our walks when it was neither too hot nor too cold. As we were walking South to North, spring was the decision. That way, the weather would hopefully improve as we progressed northwards, rather than deteriorate. The end of April seemed the optimum time to set off.

As to how long it would take, we planned on walking between 15-20 miles a day, with odd days off to catch up on our laundry, recuperate a little and perhaps clear up the blisters which we both anticipated. Our younger daughter Laura helped to crystallise matters when she announced that she was off to work in the United States in between University terms in early July. That meant we needed to finish the walk and be back in Birmingham by the end of June at the very latest. Two months to walk 900 miles? That sounded about right!

We were both in our fifties when we finally set out. Walking had been our favourite pastime for many years. We're not your stereotypical walkers, however. At the time, neither of us owned a decent pair of boots or any of the usual accoutrements associated with walking and I'm sure the purists would have looked down on us. That never worried us, however. We both loved getting out in the fresh air for an hour or two. It was our chance to blow the office cobwebs away and for us to talk about anything and everything without being interrupted by our two growing daughters.

Our usual destination was Sutton Park. It's just around the corner from our house and, at over 2,400 acres, is an absolute delight. There are woods, heath land and parkland and on a quiet day or evening you can walk for miles through beautiful surroundings, only perhaps meeting the occasional dog owner or cyclist. It wasn't always the Park, however. If it was getting dark, we'd cheerfully do a four or five mile circuit of the local streets, perhaps calling in at our local for a quick drink before returning home.

Those walks in the park seemed insignificant once we'd settled back into our seats on the train. We'd caught the 8:23 from New Street to Plymouth, where we'd get a connection to Penzance. For the first time, the enormity of what we were going to attempt struck home to me. I knew that that the walk is neatly divided into three sections by the cities of Birmingham and Glasgow. The trip down seemed to go on forever, even though I suppose we were travelling at around 80 miles an hour. If this is just a third of what we'd got in store, would we ever be able to finish it?

Perhaps in order to inspire us, the weather brightened up once we got to Plymouth. Then, once we reached Penzance, it had turned into a lovely day. We dropped our rucksacks at the bed and breakfast that we'd pre-booked and set off for the bus station in plenty of time to catch the 15:05 bus to Land's End. Or so we thought. I'd looked at the times for the Sunday service, as opposed to the weekday one and we'd just missed our bus. So much for my planning; if I couldn't get that right, what were the odds of us finishing? We retired to a nearby pub, had some late lunch and a drink and decided that if we waited for the next bus, we'd end up walking back to Penzance down country lanes in the dark. There was nothing for it but to get a taxi.

Our taxi driver was like many of his profession, pretty talkative. He soon had us telling him what we were going to attempt and told us that his son had done the trip in 24 hours, albeit by motorbike. He dropped us off at the entrance to what I suppose you'd describe as the smallish theme park that Lands End has become. We had time to have a quick look round and registered in the log that the John O'Groats to Lands End Association maintains of those attempting the challenge. We then had our pictures taken beneath the sign telling us that we had 874 miles to go and we were off on our great adventure at around 4:30.

The walk back to Penzance was just about 10 miles. This was the same distance as one of our regular training walks that we'd do at night around the perimeter of Sutton Park. We knew that this would take us about three hours. Unlike the walk around the Park, however, there were no pavements. We were walking on winding narrow country lanes and it seemed to both of us that it was uphill all the way. Maybe that was psychological; I don't know. All I do know that we were both feeling pretty bushed by the time we got to the edge of Penzance.

I've never taken much persuading to stop off at a pub. For once, Carol didn't either and we called in at "The Pirate" for something to eat before heading back to our B & B. Neither of us was very hungry and had just crab soup (delicious) and a sweet. As we got up to leave, I realised just how stiff my legs were. They loosened up as we walked the three quarters of a mile or so back to the digs but it was the first sign of something that I was going to have to get used to whenever we stopped over the days ahead.

We both had a bath but were too tired to watch TV or read. As I reflected on what was a pretty shortish first day's walk, based on the itinerary I'd planned

4

for the rest of the trip, I converted the day's mileage into a percentage of the whole journey. Just about 1% covered, 99% to go and we were already worn out. Just how far would we get? I was soon fast asleep, however, and my doubts quickly drifted away.

Day 2 Thursday 27 April 2000 Penzance to Pool

I've already said that we are not your archetypal walkers and it pretty soon became obvious that our lack of experience with rucksacks was going to be a big problem. Unlike Ian Botham, who had done the walk in the reverse direction the year before in aid of leukaemia research, we had no support team. We'd need to carry everything that we needed until we got back to the West Midlands on our backs. Clothes, spare shoes, waterproofs, first aid kits, maps, water bottles, make up (not me!); all of these were vital.

We'd finally managed to distil everything down to what we thought were the bare essentials and fitted it all into two medium sized rucksacks. What we hadn't done, however, is practise carrying a full load. That fundamental oversight had started to concern me as we walked the 200 yards from our house to the bus stop on the Wednesday morning. By the time we struggled from the station to the bed and breakfast in Penzance, the folly of it had really struck home to both of us.

After a good night's sleep and hearty breakfast, we set out at 9:30 on our first day's "real" walk. We were aiming for Redruth, our second night's destination. Our first stop, however, was the Post Office. We'd lightened the load as much as we could by removing four or five items from the rucksacks. These were duly parcelled up and sent to Alison, our older daughter, who would be holding the fort for us in Sutton Coldfield whilst we were away. . We were now really down to the bare bones but still struggled with our strange loads.

As we headed out of Penzance towards Hale via the busy A30 dual carriageway, the second culture shock hit home; there was no pavement. I'd expected this out in the country on minor roads but perhaps West Midlands' roads had spoilt us; virtually every one of them had a pavement. Not

Cornwall; now there was nothing for it, however, we just had to remember to face the oncoming traffic and stay alert.

We passed Penzance Airport, where a helicopter was just leaving for the Scilly Isles, and St Michael's Mount soon came into view. Carol took the first of what would be many photos; the sun was shining, there was a lovely breeze and I remember thinking that this was far better than being sat behind a desk. After a time, we even came across a pavement! We reached Hale in perfect time for lunch, having walked from the English Channel to the Irish Sea. Other than for a brief glimpse of it at Highbridge in Somerset, and near Morecambe Bay, this would be our last sight of the sea until, all being well, we reached the far North of Scotland.

There were plenty of places to get lunch in Hale and we eventually settled on the Harbour Café. A major consideration when we were deciding which direction to walk had been the availability of refreshments, etc en route. John O'Groats to Lands End is psychologically "downhill" and I suppose we'd have been heading towards home. However, a quick look at the map will tell you that possible refuelling stops are few and far between in Caithness and Sutherland, whereas we knew from family holidays that you were never too far from refreshments or a B & B in Cornwall and Devon. The thinking was that we'd have a good few hundred miles under our belts by the time we got to Scotland and could better manage with fewer pit stops. Not only that, we'd have the sun on our backs, as opposed to in our eyes which would have been the case had we walked from North to South. We'd also have the prevailing wind on our backs and would be following the spring, and with it the better weather, as we headed north.

Duly refreshed, we set out for Redruth via Camborne. The route seemed uphill again and it wasn't too long before Carol developed the first blister of the expedition. We'd foreseen and prepared for this and had plenty of plasters with us. Mind you, I don't think we'd anticipated getting one so early. We'd done just over 20 miles, which was no more than one of our training days and we hadn't suffered with them then. Our shoes were all well worn in and it was an unpleasant surprise to suffer from the walkers' dread so soon.

Once we had made our minds up back in Sutton Coldfield that we were definitely going to tackle the walk we knew that we would have to get down to some serious training. We'd had a couple of walking holidays in France where we'd walked from hotel to hotel but with a day's rest in between. The furthest we'd walked on one of those days was around 20 miles. Mind you, some of that was unintentional when we thought we'd lost our way and added about 6 or 7 miles to the journey.

In the three months or so prior to our departure, we began to up our usual mileage and included some walks of 15 miles or so, which would be the minimum daily distance once we set out. One of our favourites was to walk to Stonnall via Sutton Park. This was about seven and a half miles. We'd reward ourselves with a pub lunch before walking back again. Another favourite was to walk from Stratford back to the edge of Birmingham along the canal. I made a habit of taking a rucksack with me, albeit only half full, in order to get used to carrying one.

Two weeks before we set out, we did three consecutive days of 15-20 miles without suffering any ill effects and yet here we were after barely a full day's walking with blisters. Carol duly struggled on to Camborne, where we stopped for a drink. Her blisters were getting worse and she had to change her plasters. Then, as she stood up to leave and cover the last few miles to Redruth, our stop for the night, she realised that the little niggle she'd been feeling almost from the outset had turned into a full blown groin strain. Disaster! Whether it was the unusual weight of her rucksack or an awkward movement at some point, I don't know. She limped on gamely for a couple of miles but at Pool, about halfway between Camborne and Redruth, she could go no further.

We stopped for a cup of tea at Safeways Supermarket whilst we considered our options. There was no way that Carol was going to give up at such an early stage. Equally, the combination of blisters and her strain meant she could barely walk another step that night. We finally decided that there was nothing for it but to get a taxi to the B & B that we had pre-booked in Redruth.

As we talked that night I broached the subject of our agreement that if one us couldn't go on he or she would act as support for the other. Carol was adamant that it was far too early for her to think about that and she'd be carrying on. One thing was never in doubt, however. When we re-started the walk, it would have to be from exactly the same spot in Safeways in Pool. There could be no short cuts. What would be the point in that?

Day 3 Friday 28 April 200 Pool to Fraddon

One thing was quickly becoming apparent as our walk progressed, just how refreshing a cup of tea, a shower or bath and a good night's sleep can be. Carol had benefited from all three and had also re-dressed her blisters at our Redruth B & B. They were a lot easier and, although initially very stiff, her strain seemed to be at least tolerable. We had a full breakfast again and got a taxi back to last night's location, having agreed that we'd see how things went. It must have helped that the weather was lovely, a perfect spring day. We fairly soon walked the two miles or so back to Redruth and things weren't looking too bad.

Cornwall always conjures up images of picturesque coves, rugged cliffs and lonely moors. There's no way of avoiding the issue as far as Redruth is concerned, however. It was downright ugly. There was a general air of dilapidation about the town. What must have once been a hive of industry when the copper and tin mining were thriving was now generally run down and dreary. At the Post office we sent a second parcel home. Having lightened our loads to what had to be the absolute minimum, we set out for our next pre-booked accommodation at a Travel Lodge at Fraddon.

One of the first challenges we had faced once we had committed ourselves to the walk was the route. Motorways apart, you are pretty much free to walk on any road in the United Kingdom, or so I understand. As we had no pre-conceptions, the only question therefore seemed to be what would be the quickest way? As luck would have it, we soon found our answer.

One of our regular Saturday outings was to Shrewsbury, that lovely Shropshire town on the banks of the Severn. We would invariably browse the books in the charity shops that abound in the town centre and it was there that I came across a book that was to give us our route and answer many other

10

questions for us. It was called "One Man and His Dog Go Walkies" by Noel Blackham. It described how Noel and his dog Monique walked from John O'Groats to Land's End in 1988 and it gave a full description, including pitfalls of the route they had followed. All I needed to do was reverse their route, making allowances for any subsequent road building. Noel's epic journey had been commemorated at Land's End in the small exhibition of End to End memorabilia that we'd just about had time to view before setting out. There had even been a life-size cardboard model of Monique.

Again, just as luck would have it, Noel was from Birmingham. I got his number from the phone book and rang him up one night, in the hope that he wouldn't resent the intrusion and pass on a few tips. He could not have been kinder and, in addition to answering my immediate questions, he proposed that we met for a walk as he was planning a trip around Wales and needed the training.

We eventually did a couple of walks, one from Cannon Hill Park to Kings Norton and back to near Noel's house in Edgbaston and one around my local patch, Sutton Park. Sadly, Monique had passed away some time ago, so this time Noel was accompanied by his Staffordshire terrier, Guy, who would be his companion on the Welsh walk. I say accompanied by; the reality was that Guy almost dragged Noel along. Whether this made the walking any easier or not, I don't know. What was clear, however, was how great the bond of affection between man and dog was. I could easily see how Noel could not have left Monique behind when he did his long walk.

Knowing that we would be walking on roads rather than footpaths, I had bought the largest scale road map I could find and highlighted Noel's route in there. This was the Philip's Navigator book, which at a generous 1½ inches to the mile for England showed all the lanes as well as the main roads. This was to prove a godsend later in the walk, where often the original road had survived, ran more or less parallel to the new highway that had been constructed to cope with increased traffic volumes and provided a welcome relief from the traffic. This wasn't the case as far as today's walk was concerned, however. We were on the very busy A30 for most of the day and frequently ran out of pavement. There was nothing for it but to walk along the hard shoulder, facing the oncoming traffic.

We stopped for lunch at a roadside snack bar at about 1:30. Rather than just the usual small caravan with an awning, this one boasted tables and chairs and we enjoyed mugs of tea with our sausage sandwiches and muffin. There was even a WC. Not long after we set out again, Carol's blisters started giving her trouble again and she had to change the dressing again. She had also started feeling twinges in the little toe of her right foot.

We pressed on, stopping for a quick drink at a scruffy pub at Blackwater. The extra two miles that we were having to do to cater for yesterday's shortfall began to tell and the day seemed never ending. We stopped in late afternoon to fill our water bottles and soon after came across another snack bar. Our hopes of a refreshing cup of tea were soon dashed, however. He was just closing and we had to settle for the water in our bottles. It was getting cooler and we both put on the anoraks that we were carrying. Maybe it was because we were tired but at Mitchell, we made the mistake of walking down the by pass around the small town, thereby missing out on the chance of refreshments and a sit down. We were both really tired by now, so it was a great relief to come across a further roadside snack bar. Again, he was just closing but we had a cold drink and a Kit Kat each and took advantage of the WC.

At long, long last, we caught sight of the Travel Lodge near Fraddon that was our destination for the night. I've never seen a mirage but I imagine they're a bit like what we experienced then. It took an eternity to reach and even then, we had to complete a circuit off the main road to get to the entrance. Fine when you're in a car but absolute torture when you've just walked what I reckon was just about 70% of the marathon distance.

Even after a long soak in the bath, we were too tired to walk the fifty yards or so to get something to eat in the pub next door. And I was pretty sure they were showing my beloved Birmingham City on Sky Sports! Carol made a couple of phone calls and learnt that our first parcel had arrived. We then sank into the king sized bed and slept, for the first time in many years, like babies.

Day 4 Saturday 29 April 2000 Fraddon to Bodmin

Our destination for today was Bodmin. By my reckoning, this was no more than 15 miles away. Our rucksacks had been proving a real headache, so we decided to have a day off from them. Hopefully, a shorter day with no rucksacks would help recharge the batteries for both of us and clear up Carol's groin strain. We had a continental breakfast in the pub next door. I then ordered a taxi and took both packs to the B & B that we'd pre-booked at Castle Hill in Bodmin and returned to Fraddon in the same taxi, having negotiated a reduced fare for the round trip. I dare say the purists would call using a taxi cheating. Our only real rule, however, was that we'd walk every step of the way. Other than that, we were free to do as we pleased. There was nothing at all in the rules to say that we had to carry our worldly goods at all times, only that we'd walk every yard from Lands End to John O'Groats. And unlike Ian Botham, we had no support team to back us up.

Meanwhile, Carol had taken advantage of the hairdryer at the Travel Lodge and had washed her hair. We then set out at 11, along the busy A30 initially but soon finding a quieter side road that ran parallel to it. As this was to be a short day, we took our time, stopping for a drink at a pub just before re-joining the A30. By now, the main road was almost nose to tail with traffic heading for the coast for the May Day Bank Holiday. It struck us that we were probably making better speed than most of the cars but I can't honestly say that it was an enjoyable stretch of road.

At Victoria we stopped for a pub lunch of soup, potato wedges and a sour cream dip. Just before setting off I looked at the map and could see that we only had about another mile to do on the A30. At Mount Pleasant a lovely country lane provided welcome relief from the traffic and fumes we'd been

14

enduring and even saved us half a mile. Bliss! We stopped for a "quick one" at a typical country pub near Lanivet before tackling the final four-mile stretch to Bodmin. Some four-mile stretches can be a delight. This one was not, however, and it included a couple of steep hills.

By the time we reached Bodmin, the former county town of Cornwall and the only Cornish town included in the Domesday Book, Carol's little toe was very sore. We stopped at the local Boots for a dressing and also bought some postcards. The Hole in the Wall pub was nearby and we had a drink while we waited for food to be served at 6 o'clock. The wait was worthwhile, however, and the fresh crab soup was delicious.

Our bed and breakfast was a beautiful house set in a lovely garden in Castle Hill. I suppose there was a clue in the name but it never struck me when I'd booked it some months earlier. Unsurprisingly, it was up a steep hill but a cup of tea and a hot bath soon refreshed us and Carol dressed her toe which was quite inflamed by now.

We'd pre-booked bed and breakfasts as far as the Midlands. This was necessary as there was no way in which we could have carried the accommodation guides supplied by the various Tourist Boards and which listed B & B's and we wanted to be certain of accommodation at the end of our days' walks.. Accordingly, although we knew that our nights' stops would be within the town or village on our route, we hadn't appreciated just how far off the straight line a guest house or B & B might be. Even an extra half a mile at the end of a long day's walk is most frustrating. And invariably the extra half-mile seemed uphill.

Day 5 Sunday 30 April 2000 Bodmin to Kennards House

We were up quite early and had full breakfasts before setting out at 9. Mrs Morcom, our hostess, had given us directions to get back on the A30 and we soon realised that we'd have had to negotiate the hill that taxed us so much the night before anyway. Nevertheless, I'd rather have tackled it at the start of the day while my legs were still fresh than after a day on the road.

A quiet country lane took us parallel to the A30 for a mile or so before we rejoined our Nemesis just before Cardinham Down. The road was dual carriageway at this point but traffic wasn't too bad, I suppose because it was Sunday morning. We stopped at a garage for bottles of water and after another mile or so took a side road signposted for Temple. Our Phillip's Navigator Atlas showed that this was straighter than the A30, which curved at this point, and we were again glad to get off the main road.

The next 2-3 miles was glorious walking and made us glad to be alive. Ponies and cattle were everywhere, it was quiet and peaceful and there were some lovely views over Bodmin Moor. Given time, it would have been nice to explore the church of St Catherine at the tiny hamlet of Temple that we passed. This was re-built in the nineteenth century on the site of an older church that had, until 1753, been Cornwall's equivalent of Gretna Green. Marriages were conducted without banns being read or licences obtained. In earlier times, the site had apparently been home to a preceptory of the Knights Templar, hence the name of the hamlet and the nearby Temple Tor. It couldn't last, of course, and we were soon back on the main road. At around 1 o'clock we spotted Jamaica Inn, made famous in Daphne du Maurier's novel of the same name, and stopped for lunch.

I've never read the eponymous novel or seen Hitchcock's film of the same name but there was an aura about the Inn helped, I'm sure, by the displays of replica wreckers' paraphernalia from the early 19th century. By the time we'd finished our leisurely lunches (pork and turkey carveries) and drinks and had a good look at the displays and souvenirs it was 2:45 and time to get going again, stopping only to drop some post cards in the post box outside the Inn.

There was no option but to stick to the A30 for the next hour or so until we paused for mugs of tea (2 each) and cakes at a truck stop just short of the exit off the A30 for Altarnun at a place called Five Lanes. One of the benefits of 5 or 6 hours walking with full back packs each day was that we seemed able to eat what we wanted with impunity. If anything, I was losing weight, so managed to convince myself that I needed to load up on calories. It didn't take long...

Looking at our trusty road atlas I could see that one of the five lanes mirrored a curve in the A30 at this juncture and would take us to a point just a mile or so short of our next overnight stop at Kennards House without adding many, if any, miles to our day's walk. Just as in the morning, we were rewarded with 5 miles or so of tranquil, scenic walking, albeit up and down hill in parts. We had the road to ourselves, seemingly, and crossed several streams including the River Inny, a tributary of the River Tamar. That latter name registered as forming the boundary between Cornwall and Devon and I knew that at some point tomorrow we would have traversed the length of Cornwall, a palpable achievement. We only had a mile or so of the A30 to negotiate and soon arrived at Trethorne Leisure Farm at Kennards House. A nearby road sign said that it was 19 miles to Bodmin, so we allowed ourselves slightly self-satisfied smiles as we ended a mainly enjoyable and eventful day's walking.

Nobody seemed around at the farm, which caters for family holidays and allows children to feed the animals, etc. It also includes a golf course. Mrs Davey, the landlady, had left a note explaining that we were in room 6 and that the doors were not locked so we went straight up, had a refreshing cup of tea and I had an even more refreshing shower. Bliss!

Not long afterwards, Mrs Davey returned and kindly made us another cup of tea which we had in the lounge with some of her home-made biscuits. More bliss, and for once it was Carol that ate too many. We also spotted a copy of Noel Blackham's book that I'd "lifted" our route from. Mrs Davey remembered both Noel and his dog Monique and explained that Noel had sent her the book.

Once we'd adjourned to our room, Carol had a bath and we settled down to watch TV in bed. We agreed that, even though we had our packs to carry once more, today had been the most enjoyable so far, particularly the stretch around Temple. Carol revealed that her blisters and other ailments, particularly her groin strain, were all improving and we both enjoyed a really good night's sleep. As I drifted off, I calculated that we'd done nearly 80 miles so far and only had 820 or so to go. That sort of visualization of a problem or timescale in percentage terms has always been one of my coping strategies; it particularly helped when I got to 50% of a task completed and told myself that all I had to do was the same again and that would be job done. And of course once I passed half way, the percentage remaining to be done decreased rapidly in proportion to the amount done.

I used to drive my colleagues at Birmingham City Council to distraction in early 1998 when I started a daily countdown to when I'd take voluntary redundancy from a job I'd grown to hate. Sorry, guys! So just another 10 times what we'd done so far and we'd be at John O'Groats. Simple.

Day 6 Monday 1 May 2000 Kennards House to Bridestowe

This was a really glorious morning; the sort of English Spring day that would make anyone glad to be alive and free, like we were, to enjoy it in any way that they wanted. We had our breakfasts in the lounge at Trethorne Farm, taking in the lovely views as we ate. By 9 am we were back on the road again, having for the first time on our journey had to apply sun screen lotion to arms, necks and faces. As we set out, however, I noticed that one of the two pairs of shoes I'd been so careful to "walk in" on our training days was beginning to show signs of wear and obviously wouldn't last much longer. This was a little disquieting as I'd planned to use these two pairs all the way. Ah well...

After an hour or so of mainly quiet side roads we reached Launceston, the ancient capital of Cornwall and a charming market town. We stopped at the White Hart Hotel for a cup of tea. It was Mayday Bank Holiday Monday, so not many of the local shops were open. We found a Safeway supermarket that was, however, and bought sandwiches, water and bananas for lunch. Our Navigator Atlas showed that thankfully we could avoid the dreaded A30 and we left Launceston via the A388. It didn't take too long to reach the local rugby club and immediately after that a bridge took us and the road over the River Tamar and into Devon. We'd conquered our first county and shared a moment of muted yet tangible triumph as I took a picture of Carol sat on the bridge wall. Perhaps, just perhaps, we might reach John O'Groats?

The A388 then took us on to Lifton where we ate our lunches and had a quick "livener" in the Court House Pub. Very refreshing, and we needed it because set us up for what was to be a tough afternoon. We were now walking on what I believe to be the old route into and out of Cornwall before the dual carriageway which is the modern A30 was created. In any event, we referred to it as the "old" A30 and initially it was ideal for our purposes, running parallel as it more or less did to the new version. There was a footpath all the way, very little traffic and stunning views over Dartmoor on our right hand side. But my word it was long, and whilst perhaps not as winding as Paul McCartney's was, it was certainly rolling! That latter word is often used to describe the British countryside and, viewed from afar, conjurers up an almost idyllic image of gentle slopes in various shades of green. When you're walking about 10 miles of it with heavy packs, however, the reality is nothing but uphill and downhill. And by now the wind had got up and seemed to be directly in our faces. The euphoria of the morning was rapidly fading

We paused for a cup of tea at Lewdown, half way between Lifton and Bridestowe, then pressed on. At long last we arrived at Bridestowe at about 6 o'clock, only to find that our B&B for the night at Week Farm was another ½ a mile or so out of the town and, true to form, a further ¾ of a mile up a steep road to the west. At long, long last we arrived and Mrs Margaret Hockridge and her husband made us very welcome and gave us a lovely tea of pasties, sandwiches, scones and jam and cream whilst we sat in their lounge telling them about our adventure. We were worn out, however, after what was, we thought, our longest day to date and soon headed for our room for showers and bed.

As we relaxed in bed we talked of how tiring the day had been. The strong headwind in the afternoon had affected Carol's eyes and that and that, coupled with the weight of our rucksacks left us feeling a bit down. Carol in particular was suffering from a recurrence of her groin strain and had no doubt that it was attributable to the load she was unaccustomed to carrying.

At an early stage in planning the walk I'd mooted two possibilities as alternatives to carrying all our worldly goods on our backs. One was to look for a support driver but we fairly quickly dismissed that idea as impractical.

The other was to use two vehicles in a kind of "ferrying" arrangement. My idea was to get a camper van and a moped or small motor bike. Each morning, I'd put the bike in the camper van, head off for the next night's stop, park up and come back to Carol on the bike with just a small rucksack containing our map and waterproofs. We'd then do our day's walk relatively unencumbered, go back in the camper to our previous location, collect the bike, head back up the road and sleep in the van or a B&B. All that we had to ensure was that we didn't cut corners and walked every step of the way. Just as with the idea of a support driver, we eventually dismissed the ferrying concept and opted to carry everything in rucksacks. But after almost a week it was now obvious that our chances of success and enjoyment were being affected by having to carry big packs; we had to re-think.

Our family car was due for an upgrade and I'd got in mind to trade it in when we finished our walk. What if, when we got to Birmingham, we bought our next car without a trade-in, I proposed to Carol? We'd then have two cars available for the "ferrying" operation for the rest of the walk and I could sell the old one privately when we got back from Scotland. The more we talked, the more attractive the idea seemed. We could take as many clothes, shoes, maps, and tourist information guides as we wanted. All we'd need to carry each day was a small pack containing essentials such as maps, waterproofs and lunch. In addition, around well populated areas, we could probably use public transport to get back to our previous night's location in the morning. In that way, we wouldn't have to return to collect a car at night.

Our idea had always been to do the walk for our own satisfaction, not to meet anyone else's sniffy assumptions about how long distance walking should be done. Before long, we'd convinced ourselves that this was what we'd do from Birmingham onwards and we drifted off to sleep confident that if we could just get back to Brum with our packs than we'd have an excellent chance of reaching our final destination.

Day 7 Tuesday 2 May 2000 Bridestowe to Okehampton

As ever, a good night's sleep refreshed us. A transport map of Devon in our room showed that there was a train line from Taunton to Highbridge, which would be our walk for the coming Saturday, and it struck us that we could use the train to initially take our rucksacks. We also knew that today was going to be a short day of only 6 miles or so as we planned to catch up with laundry, etc. at Okehampton. Our mood was even further improved when, over breakfast, Mrs Hockridge, who must have seen how low we had been the night before, offered to take our rucksacks to Okehampton for us. We accepted with thanks, needless to say, and eventually set out unburdened for what would be a stroll compared to the last few days.

The route took us along the "old" A30 for a mile or two, then we re-joined the new A30 dual carriageway version for half a mile or so to a place called Meldon, where we took the road to Okehampton. From Meldon, the A30 and its four busy lanes of traffic heads east. Our route from now on would be north east and I can't say we were sorry to see the back of our old foe!

Our usual walking pace was 10 miles or so every three hours, so within two hours we were in Okehampton. Although it was a relatively small town of 6-7,000 people there were plenty of shops, including a shoe shop. I took the opportunity to buy some trainers as my one pair of shoes were now completely useless. Carol found a chemist and bought Optrex eye drops as her eyes were still giving her trouble and some more plasters for the inevitable blisters. She also spotted some wraparound sun glasses that she thought might give her eyes some protection from the wind but eventually decided against buying them. We then bought a couple of papers and adjourned to the Plume of Feathers for a leisurely pub lunch.

Two hours later (I said it was leisurely!) we set out for our B & B for the night in Station Road, passing a laundrette on the way. Our rucksacks had been safely delivered by Mrs Hockridge and Carol sorted out what needed washing before heading off to the laundrette that we had passed. Once she returned, we decided that we could, after all, lighten our loads even more and made up a third parcel to send home. We had showers before I went and bought some date and apricot flapjacks for our tea. In the meantime, Carol rested up on the bed, trying to ease the groin strain that was still troubling her. We watched one of our favourite TV programmes, University Challenge, at 8 and were asleep soon afterwards.

Day 8 Wednesday 3 May 2000 Okehampton to Crediton

We were up at 8 and over breakfast got talking to a Dutch girl who was travelling alone. She was setting up a business delivering flowers to England and, like most Dutch people I'd ever come across, she spoke excellent English. By now, Carol was getting fed up of a full English breakfast each morning and decided she'd limit herself to toast and cereals for a while. I, on the other hand, made no such commitment…

The weather forecast for today was cloudy but no rain. It was pretty cool, however, so we added an extra layer of clothes to our usual outfits. We soon set out, pausing at the Post Office on Station Road to send our latest, and surely last, parcel home. I ditched my old shoes in a bin together with one of our water bottles that had developed a broken catch and soon afterwards we found the B3215 signposted for Crediton. This was another long and winding Devon country road without footpaths but there wasn't much traffic and it felt good to be on our way once more. And by now we'd learned that cooler weather was far preferable to hot when it came to long distance walking, just so long as it was dry.

At 11:20, and after 51/2 miles of walking, we came to a pub called "The Countryman". Despite there being a sign that promised it opened at 11, and much to our disappointment, it was shut. We carried on along the A3072, arriving at a village called Bow, some 41/2 miles and an hour and a half later. Here we stopped at an old pub called The White Hart. A young lad aged about 18 served us to drinks and crisps but could offer no food as his mother, who did the cooking, had gone out. He did however tell us where we could get something to eat at the village shop a little further on up the street.

As we enjoyed our drinks we noticed a picture of Sir Ian Botham on the pub wall. He was accompanied by Gary Lineker and the picture showed Sir Ian walking through Bow in 1999 on the way to Lands End from John O'Groats. This was the second time that Sir Ian had done the walk, raising millions for leukaemia research in the process. I'd like to digress for just a moment if I may. Ten years later I was sat in my back garden one weekend reading a newspaper when I heard something of a commotion in the road outside. There was a band playing and obviously something going on so I put my paper down and wandered out to the front garden. It was Sir Ian Botham and a large entourage. He was still fundraising for leukaemia research, this time doing a series of city based walks. Seeing that I'd been diagnosed with leukaemia a couple of years earlier I thought that the least I could do was put something in the collecting bucket and put in a tenner, which was all that I had on me. He smiled and said "Thank you sir" and I thought what a decent bloke. He'd given up yet more of his time to raise funds for people like me and all I could do was sit in the garden. And he called me "Sir" when of course it should have been me calling him that for his contribution to cricket and charity.

We left the White Hart after half an hour or so and soon found the village shop where we bought warm Cornish pasties and ate them sat on a wall outside. Not long after Bow our Navigator Atlas came up trumps with a country lane that looked more direct than the A3072 and A377 that would have been the alternative. There was no traffic at all on this road and we were able to enjoy 5 or 6 miles of care free walking, passing through a hamlet called Coleford en route before re-joining the A377 for the last 2-3 miles into Crediton. By now, the local rush hour was approaching and we had to take great care on what was a single carriageway road with plenty of fast traffic.

I'm sure Crediton had seen better days but it struck both of us as, putting it kindly, a little frayed at the edges. We found a café that was still serving and had some tea, pausing to ring our B & B for the night to let them know we'd be there about 6. The café owner gave us directions to Old Tiverton Road where we were staying and we set off for the last time. Sure enough, Longview, our B & B, was at the top of yet another hill. I suppose that we could have inferred that from the name and to be fair, there was a lovely view from our bedroom. Mr King, our host, made us a cup of tea in the lounge but we soon retired to our room to unwind. Once again, a warm bath did both of us the world of good. Carol rang home to say bon voyage to Laura, our younger daughter, who was going back to Swansea University the next day. Laura told us that our last parcel had arrived and also the photo that we'd had taken beneath the signpost at Lands End. As usual, we talked over the events of the day and Carol wrote up her notebook. We had a brief chat over the route for the following day and soon nodded off.

Day 9 Thursday 4 May 2000 Crediton to Sampford Peverell

Mr and Mrs King, our hosts at Crediton, were, like most landlords and landladies we stayed with, lovely people. Not only did they include eggs from chickens in the garden in our breakfasts but Mrs King told us she was off to see her mother-in-law in Sampford Peverell that day and would take our packs for us. I'd worked out that today would be 20 miles or so; again, it didn't take us long to accept her kind offer.

We set out at 9:30 along the A3072 heading for Tiverton, the next town on our route. It was cool, windy and very hilly but the absence of packs and lovely views of the Devon countryside more than made up for those conditions. After 8 ½ miles, which took over 3 hours because of the hilly going, we came to a place called Bickleigh. If ever there was the epitome of a chocolate box setting, this was it. Thatched cottages, a medieval stone bridge, a medieval church and the confluence of the rivers Exe and Dart made it an archetypal Devon village. And there was a pub! The Fisherman's Cot was set on the river bank, had a decent menu and enabled us to pass a very pleasant couple of hours.

It was a little reluctantly that we set out again after a really lovely, relaxing lunch for Tiverton on the A3072 but at least we had regular views of the River Exe for company. Not long after we left, a passing white car pipped us. It was Mrs King, returning from Sampford Peverell and we both gave grateful waves. As we approached Tiverton, the volume and speed of the traffic increased and we had to take great care on what was a single carriageway road with many bends and no footpaths. It didn't take too long however before we were on the outskirts of the town and the pavement started.

All I knew of Tiverton was that it was one of the "Rotten Boroughs" that until the 19th century returned 2 Members of Parliament for what were relatively small populations. Apparently, just 400 electors had the vote and there was no secret ballot. Mind you, that compared favourably with Old Sarum, precursor to the neighbouring and newer Salisbury, which returned 2 MP's from an electorate of 7. At the same time, Manchester had no MP of its own, forming part of the Lancashire constituency. How things have changed…

In the town centre, I decided to get some new trainers as I had a largish blister on my heel, this time in a size 10 ½ to see if that would help ease the problem. Carol bought herself some of the wraparound sunglasses that she'd first spotted in Okehampton because her eyes were still giving her problems in the wind. We stopped off at the Tourist Information Centre to collect a town map and the helpful lady who served us showed us the Grand Western Canal that went from Tiverton to Sampford Peverell, our destination. She explained that the canal was a country park and a nature reserve. This sounded ideal; canals were invariably on the level, there would be no traffic and we could end the day in a lovely environment.

We paused as we joined the canal towpath so that I could put a fresh plaster on my heel and change into my new trainers. The TIC woman had been right and we enjoyed a lovely hour or so until we came to a village called Halberton. Our Pathfinder map showed that the canal took a biggish loop of about a mile or so. We decided to take the short cut through the village and soon came across The Barge, the local pub. This, we decided, was too serendipitous an opportunity to forgo so we went in! We had smoked salmon sandwiches for our tea, a leisurely drink and read the daily papers, one of our favourite pastimes.

Suitably refreshed, we re-joined the canal for the last couple of miles or so to Sampford Peverell. We quickly found our B & B for the night, not uphill for once, where Mrs Isaacs made us a cup of tea and gave us biscuits. We both had baths but even though there was a pub next door, decided against going out again. As usual, we talked over the day and did a bit of planning for our next destination, Taunton. As we talked, I realised that by tomorrow night we'd have "done" Devon and approximately one sixth of our long walk would be behind us. We were getting there…

Day 10 Friday 5 May 2000 Sampford Peverell to Taunton

We had breakfast at 8 and were back on the road by 8:45 on what was quite a cool morning. The A38, our route for today, soon crossed the M5 and I was grateful that this busy 1960's motorway had taken all but local traffic away from the road we were now travelling. There was, thankfully, pavement for most of the way and we made good progress. After about two hours we came to a pub called the Poacher's Pocket at a place called Burlescombe. The door was locked but just as we were about to leave a girl came to the door and said we were welcome to come in. We had a coffee each, read the morning papers and were back on the road by 11:15. Welcome as these breaks were, I was finding that my legs would stiffen up and that it would take five minutes or so for me to get back into my usual walking rhythm.

We stayed on the A38 until the outskirts of Wellington then took a road signposted for the town centre. As we reached the centre, we got chatting to a woman called Marina who was heading the same way. When she found out what we were doing, she seemed fascinated. She thought we must be celebrities of sorts and said she'd look out for us on the news. I hope she wasn't too disillusioned when we didn't appear!

In the town we bought a couple of papers and settled down to a leisurely lunch of fish and chips at the King's Arms pub. By my reckoning, we had upped our daily calorific intake by about 50% since starting out but it didn't seem to matter as we were walking it off, helped no doubt by the weight of our backpacks. I weighed myself whenever I got the chance and for the first time in years saw that I was gradually losing weight. Before we left, we got talking to one of the waitresses who could not believe that we were about to walk the 7 miles or so to Taunton. Little did she realise…

At 2:45 we headed out of town, quickly picking up the A38 once more. The sun was now out and we stopped to take off our anoraks as it was quite warm. At the edge of Taunton we rang our B&B for the night for directions. These were straightforward and we arrive at 5 to be greeted with cups of tea and biscuits. Even though, at just under 15 miles, this had been one of our shorter days it was great to put our feet up and relax.

By 6 we were ready for something more substantial to eat and found a pub called the Rat and Parrot not too far away. I gathered that this was one of a chain of pubs all with the same name and operated by Scottish and Newcastle Breweries. It suited our needs, however, and got back to the B&B at 8 suitably refreshed and replenished.

Just as in virtually all of our overnight stops there was a television in our room and we watched Have I Got News For You and read for a while. Carol then had a text message from her friend Selina. As I'm writing this quite a few years after the event that seems a mundane thing to note; she receives and sends hundreds a week nowadays. But at that time it was a novelty for her and she spent quite a time composing her reply. We chatted over the events of the day as usual, discussed tomorrow and were soon fast asleep.

Day 11 Saturday 6 May 2000 Taunton to Highbridge

After another 8am breakfast we set out on our day's adventure at 9. We stopped in the town centre to top up on our plasters' stash and bought postcards and stamps. Throughout the journey we'd been updating family and friends on our progress, always including Noel Blackham who had been such an inspiration to us. We had to seek directions for the A38, our road for the whole of the day, from a man on a bike. His advice was to catch a bus as it was a mile or two and couldn't believe we were walking. I didn't tell him our ultimate destination…

After about three hours and ten miles of fairly hard going along the A38 without much in the way of pavement and only really interspersed with a stop at a garage for bottles of water we came to a place called North Petherton. Our landlady at Taunton had recommended a pub called "The Walnut Tree" which we duly found. Just in time! The heavens opened and we had our first thunderstorm since setting out. We relaxed with the morning papers over a long, delicious and, I confess, boozy lunch and decided to have an afternoon without our packs.

I've said before that we wanted to enjoy our trip of a lifetime and that it shouldn't be an ordeal so we got a taxi to Highbridge, our next stop, got the driver to wait whilst I dropped the packs off and collected a key (the very trusting landlady said she might be out when we got there in the evening) and drove back to North Petherton, arriving at about 3:15. By now, as often happens after a thunderstorm, it was lovely and sunny. We carried on along the A38, avoiding Bridgwater town centre, crossed the River Parrett and stopped at a pub at 4:45 just in time to watch the football results over something cold and refreshing!

The remaining 5 miles or so into Highbridge were pretty flat and mainly along footpaths. This was just as well as our feet were aching after a fairly full day. The little toe on my left foot was particularly painful and I feared something other than the ubiquitous blister. We stopped at a garage and bought yoghurts and Kit Kats to have with a cup of tea in our bedroom and finally arrived at our bed and breakfast accommodation at 7:45 pm.

Mrs Ingram, the landlady, could not have been nicer. She made us cups of tea and gave us cakes and was, in many ways, just like my late mother. In fairness, most of our hosts had been lovely, with the exception of one gentleman who had something of the Norman Bates, of Psycho fame, about him but Mrs Ingram was my favourite to date. We had baths and retired to bed to catch up on our post card duties. It was at this point that I realised, or thought I realised, that what had been troubling my left foot was a corn on the little toe. I'd had many of these over the years, however, and wasn't too troubled, deciding that I'd get some corn plasters as soon as possible.

Our next night was to be spent with Carol's sister Judy and her husband Doug at their house at Nailsea. This was just of our route but they'd kindly agreed to pick us up somewhere on the route in the evening and drop us back off at the same place the following morning. Carol rang Doug to finalise arrangements and they agreed that we'd also meet up somewhere convenient for lunch the following day. Carol said she'd ring him again in the morning to finalise arrangements and we soon drifted off to sleep.

Day 12 Sunday 7 May 2000 Highbridge to Felton

We both slept well and had breakfast at 8 again. Carol borrowed a hairdryer from Mrs Ingram and washed her hair. Being folically challenged can have advantages on occasions; I just wash and go when it comes to that job! Mrs Ingram told us that she was doing a five mile sponsored walk in aid of Save The Children today, so I sponsored her for a fiver. It was the least I could do as she'd been most welcoming. Carol rang Judy and arranged that we would meet her and Doug at a pub near Winscombe on the A38. The weather forecast was for a hot day and the sun was already shining brightly as we set out at 9:15.

Once more we were walking along the A38, the main road to the West Country for Brummies such as us until the M5 was built. We soon passed Brent Knoll, a prominent isolated hill on our left, buying bottles of water, which we knew we'd need on such a warm day, at a nearby garage. The going was, thankfully, quite flat and we soon crossed the busy M5 just south of Sedgemoor Services. Around 1pm, and after about ten miles, we came to a sign pointing to Winscombe, which was ¼ of a mile downhill on a road to our left. Carol thought that Judy and Doug might have gone down there, so we made our way down to a pub called The Woodborough, albeit somewhat grudgingly on my part. It was hot, the little toe on my left foot was by now causing me quite some grief and I resented any detour, however minimal, on such a warm day.

There was no sign of Doug and Judy, so we had a couple of drinks and some lunch. Carol had been trying to phone them but got no answer. Every now and then she had a look outside but there was no sign of them. Than at around 2:30 we had a call from them. They'd been looking for us along the A38 and had driven through Winscombe but not thought to go in the pub we were in. We told them that we would stay where we were until 3:00 then walk back up to the A38.

Having walked back up the hill in what was by now really warm weather we finally met up with Doug and Judy. They took our rucksacks (Thank God!) and agreed to pick us up at Felton, which is just past Bristol Airport at about 6pm. Thankfully, we now enjoyed a very flat stretch of the A38 until, and after two refuelling stops for water and cups of tea, we came to a gradual but seemingly eternal hill at Redhill. By now I reckoned we'd walked the best part of 200 miles but had yet to acquire a taste for hills, particularly when it was hot and one of us, me in this case, had a foot problem. Finally, finally, the road levelled out and we came to Bristol Airport just in time to see a Boeing 737 take off directly over our heads. Such is the proximity of the airport to the A38 that the road has to be closed to traffic for take offs and landings.

We got to Felton at 6:15, phoned Judy and Doug and they picked us up after 5 minutes. Having had a bath, me, and a shower, Carol, we had a really lovely tea. Doug told me that Birmingham City, our mutual favourite football team, had drawn their final match of the season, thus ensuring a place in the play-offs for promotion to the Premiership. Even that news, and the great meal, couldn't take my mind off my toe, however. It really was hurting, far more so than the usual corns and blisters that I'd experienced before. I was still dwelling on it as we went to bed, having first rung home to check that all was well. For the first time since we set out I had real doubts that I could make it to John O'Groats…

Interlude 8-12th May 2000

When I woke on the morning of Monday 8th May it was pretty clear that I wouldn't be walking far that day, or for a few more days come to that. The little toe on my left foot was full of what I assumed was pus and swollen to at least twice its normal size. Judy managed to get me an appointment at her GP's surgery and I was duly seen at 11:30. The diagnosis was a septic toe, possibly caused by a substance in the corn plasters I'd been using, and I was prescribed antibiotics and a few days of minimal walking.

Having gathered our thoughts back at Judy's, we decided to go home and regroup. We booked tickets on the 4:30 coach from Bristol to Birmingham and Judy dropped us off in Bristol city centre, having done some lunch for us. We'd already decided to implement our Plan B option of using two cars in a ferrying arrangement from Bristol onwards so I used the waiting time for our coach to go into the Bristol branch of my bank and arrange a loan for our new car. By 7pm we were back home, having got a taxi from Digbeth Coach Station in Birmingham.

Although initially a little deflated to be home sooner than anticipated, there was never any doubt in either of our minds that this would only be a temporary interval. We had walked nearly 200 miles, carrying all our worldly goods on our backs for most of them. We knew that blisters could be overcome, that our trusty Phillip's Navigator map had proved invaluable in keeping us on the right track and off main roads if possible and that however tired we might be after a day's walk there was nothing that a cup of tea and a bath or shower couldn't put right.

Admittedly, the ferrying of cars in the mornings and evenings would be a nuisance but there were so many plusses that we took little convincing of this option. I anticipated that this would add around an hour each way at most to our day's itinerary but we were only walking for about six hours each day. We could take all the clothes, including rainwear, shoes and accommodation guides that we could possibly need. We could also use the morning journey to reconnoitre our day's walk, noting potential pit stops and tricky roads for pedestrians. I anticipated that this might be problematical once we got to parts of Scotland, for example, where refreshment stops would be few and far between. In addition, we could see that around the big cities we would be negotiating it would be possible to take the cars on to our next night's accommodation and get public transport back to our previous night's halt. Again, the proviso would have to be that we started walking at exactly our finishing point from the night before.

On the Tuesday, 9th May, I bought our new car. We used the following couple of days in making sure that all of our equipment was up to scratch, including waterproofs and footwear; after all, the only constraint would be what we could fit into the one "day" rucksack that I planned to carry. I had already "walked in" two pairs of shoes in anticipation of changing them in Birmingham, which was one third of the way on our journey, so these were packed as a welcome alternative to the trainers that I'd been wearing. We re-visited our planned itinerary to make sure that we could still be home from Scotland before our daughter Laura set out for the United States. Initially, we had factored in periodic rest days to catch up with laundry, etc., and in case of blisters. These went and we were confident that we could still meet that deadline, albeit just about.

By the Thursday, the antibiotics had done their thing and my toe was visibly improving and free from pain. I re-arranged accommodation that we had pre-booked, more or less at the same locations and on Friday 12th May 2000 we set out in two cars for another night at Judy and Doug's; the adventure was back on!

Day 13 Saturday 13 May 2000 Felton to Alveston

As we set out from Judy and Doug's the weather forecast for the day ahead was warm. We drove to Alveston, which is North of Bristol and not to be confused with Olveston, a mile down the road from Alveston, and left a car outside the Bridleway B & B, our home for the night. By 11am we were back at Felton, the spot where Judy and Doug had picked us up on the previous Sunday evening, and ready to resume our challenge.

After a couple of miles on the A38 we stopped at the Fox and Goose for a drink. We were no longer burdened down by heavy packs but were feeling the heat and were very thirsty. Carrying on, we crossed Bedminster Bridge into Bristol City, the biggest conurbation we'd encountered so far on our walk. Were it not for the distinctive Bristolian accent, we could have been in Birmingham, so familiar looking was the environment. We carried on through Bristol, stopping at the Fish Market pub just across Bristol Bridge for lunch. We didn't rush, taking time to read the papers because we knew that we were in for a long, hot afternoon and finally got underway again at 3pm.

By now it was very warm and we were delighted not to be carrying big packs. We passed through Filton, renowned for its aerospace connection, centred on its airport, and home of the inaugural Concorde flight. We walked through Patchway, pausing at a pub to quench our thirsts. Sadly for me, this turned into drowning my sorrows as I found out that my beloved Blues had lost 4-0 to Barnsley in the first leg of the Division 1 play-offs, thereby effectively ending any chance of promotion to the Premiership. Mind you, stoicism comes easy to Blues fans; we have been promoted and relegated more times than any other Football league club. And at least the man we were talking to in the pub liked Blues fans as they were nice when visiting his team, Bristol Rovers. This wasn't a lot of consolation, however…

Almondsbury came next before we finally arrived at Alveston at 7:45 after our longest day's walk to date of just over 21 miles. My toe had survived intact but the ubiquitous blisters had re-emerged. I dressed them and, after a refreshing cup of tea, we set off back to Felton to retrieve the first car. We agreed that, on balance, this was far preferable to carrying all our worldly goods on our backs and were back in Alveston at 9:45, just in time to watch the voting in the Eurovision Song Contest. The winners were Denmark, via the Olsen Brothers, with the instantly forgettable "Fly On The Wings Of Love". Whatever happened to them, I wonder? Sic transit gloria mundi, indeed!

Day 14 Sunday 14 May 2000 Alveston to Quedgeley

We were up for breakfast at 8 and could see straightaway that we were in for another hot day. Mrs Wenger, our hostess, was very chatty and interested in our walk and my plans to write this book. In turn, she showed us the book she had written for her grandchildren about her cat, "Gorky" and his friend "Smudge". Carol and I were both impressed.

By 8:45 we were underway in our 2 cars to Lower Green Farm at Haresfield, our next overnight stop. This turned out to be about 2 miles off the A38, the longest deviation off our route that we had had to make for accommodation. Mr Reed, our host for the night, was also, like Mrs Wenger, very interested in our walk and quickly came up with a plan that would save time and our legs at the end of the day. He was on the Committee of Gloucestershire County Cricket Club and just about to set off for Cardiff, where his team were playing Glamorgan. He'd be happy to drop us off at Alveston if we could wait 5 minutes. Needless to say we jumped at the chance as we knew we were in for another long, hot day.

We left one car on his drive and followed him back to the car park of the Little Chef café back on the A38. Leaving our other car there, ready to pick up on the evening, we joined him in his and he dropped us off at traffic lights in Alveston, just 25 yards from where we had finished our walk the night before. As ever, we walked back those 25 yards, there could be no cheating, and were ready to head north again by 10:45.

After a warm but pretty uneventful 6 miles or so we stopped for lunch at the Berkeley Vale Pub. We enjoyed a typical Sunday meal of roast beef followed by a nice pudding; all very relaxing and we were tempted to stop and watch the play-off game between Bolton and Ipswich. Duty called, however, and we were back on the all too warm road again by 2:15.

We topped up our water supplies at a garage and pressed on. At 4:30 we came to another pub. Much to our disappointment, this was closed but we finally found one open at 4:55 and stopped for shandies and crisps. Leaving at 5:30 on what was a very warm May evening we finally made it back to the Little Chef where we had left our car at 8, absolutely worn out after a second consecutive 21 mile day.

We had a cup of tea and read the papers at the Little Chef before making our way back to Lower Green Farm, a really lovely farmhouse. Gloucester and Glamorgan had drawn, so Mr Reed's trip had been worthwhile. After baths, we relaxed by watching the national news followed by the local news, which was the Central version, the same as we get at home in Birmingham. We must be back in the Midlands, I thought, although I found out the next morning that Mrs Reed did not like to be thought of as a Midlander. After watching Match Of The Day, we had a really good night's sleep, our reward I felt for a really hard day on the road.

Day 15 Monday May 15 2000 Quedgeley to Tewkesbury

Another warm day; after an 8am breakfast we set out in our two cars to look for overnight accommodation in Tewkesbury, our destination for the day. It had been the one place that we had not been able to pre-book when back in Birmingham waiting for my toe to heal. Luckily, the first B&B we came to on the A38 had a twin room for the night and room for our cars so we booked in, left a car there and drove back to the Little Chef café where we had finished our walk the previous night.

After a mile or so on the A38, we turned off onto the quieter A4330, stopping after a short while for a "refresher" in a pub. Well, it was a very hot day! We carried on towards Gloucester, pausing only to buy bottles of water, until we reached the City Centre. I have to say that the City seemed particularly run down to us. Perhaps it was just the parts we saw? We didn't come across the Cathedral, for example, which looks magnificent in the pictures I have seen. Having said that, it is the burial place of King Edward II. Details of his murder, allegedly involving a red hot poker, have always sent a shiver down my spine, so maybe it was as well we missed it. Or maybe we were influenced by the notoriety it had acquired six years earlier as the home to Fred and Rose West, serial killers of 12 women and girls between them, including two of their own daughters? They lived in Cromwell Street and for weeks on end in the mid 90's it featured on the evening news as their garden and house was searched exhaustively, unfortunate victims being unearthed on a seemingly daily basis. By the time we walked through Gloucester, the house had been demolished, not that we had any interest in seeing it.

We bought post cards, plasters, again, and some thinner socks for Carol before having a leisurely lunch at the New Inn pub in the centre of Gloucester. By 3pm we were back on the road. The afternoon was pretty uneventful, interrupted only by stops for water and to take advantage of the occasional bench or bus stop with seats that we came across. My blisters were playing up a lot and I was glad of the rest, however brief. We reckoned we had about 2 miles to go when we came across the Swan pub and would have loved to have stopped for a quick one but it wasn't going to be open until Wednesday! Heaven knows how the local alcoholics manage. Shortly afterwards, we passed the spot where we'd seen some New Age Travellers, complete with horses, earlier in the day as we ferried the cars. They had gone now but we knew, much to our relief, that we only had a mile or so to go for the day.

By 6pm we were at our destination. Cups of tea and baths helped us to recover and we watched the news and weather as we recuperated. Carol realised that she had left her address book in the New Inn pub and I realised that I had left my fleece jacket somewhere. We set off to recover our second car from the Little Chef at 7:45, stopping en route at the New Inn pub. Much to Carol's relief, her address book was there and we continued on our way. At the Little Chef, I phoned Mrs Wenger, our hostess at Alveston. She confirmed that she had my fleece and somewhat reluctantly I decided to go and collect it. Carol took advantage of the facilities at the Little Chef and enjoyed a cup of tea and a toasted teacake until I re-joined her 45 minutes later. Somewhat chastened, we drove in convoy back to Tewkesbury, vowing to be more careful in future.

Day 16 Tuesday 16 May 2000 Tewkesbury to Kempsey

This was a red letter day; we would be sleeping in our own bed tonight! Noel Blackham, our mentor, had planned his journey to incorporate an overnight stop at his home in Edgbaston, Birmingham on his way southwards. This involved a somewhat circular route from Stafford to Worcester using the A34 and A38. However, I could see that the A449, to the west of Birmingham, linked those two towns and was a far straighter road. From my training walks with Noel, and based on the distances he did each day when he did the walk, I knew that his pace was appreciably greater than ours so he was probably not overly fussed at the extra mileage. It mattered to us, however; we couldn't do 30+ miles a day like Noel often did. I also knew that there were excellent train and bus links from the A449 to our home in Sutton Coldfield and that we could save on the not inconsiderable cost of bed and breakfasts for a few nights by careful planning.

We had breakfast at 8 and spent some time chatting to Mr and Mrs Durn, our hosts. They weren't worried by the New Age Travellers that we'd seen but roundly condemned the gypsies that were encamped in a nearby lane as nuisances and thieves. So much for the glamour of life on the road. By 9:30 we were underway in the cars, stopping after 14 miles or so at a village called Kempsey, on the A38 just before Worcester. The landlord of the Anchor Inn was happy for us to leave a car there and I told him that we'd undoubtedly be partaking of one or two after our day's walk. By 10:50 we were back at Tewkesbury, left the other car there and set out northwards once more.

Our previous night's stopover was actually a couple of miles short of the centre of Tewkesbury, so we set out at a fairly leisurely pace towards the town. We stopped at the refectory at Tewkesbury Abbey for tea and home-made cakes; lovely. After the Battle of Tewkesbury in the Wars of the Roses in May 1471, some of the defeated Lancastrians sought sanctuary in the Abbey. The victorious Yorkists, led by King Edward IV, forced their way into the abbey; the resulting bloodshed caused the building to be closed for a month until it could be purified and re-consecrated. It all seemed very tranquil now, however.

By 12 we were back walking and carried on without further pauses until we came to the Bluebell pub at 13:55, just in time for last orders for lunch. En route, we crossed from Gloucestershire to Worcestershire. It was quite warm but there was a pleasant breeze blowing, the scenery was lovely and we could see the Malvern Hills, home to many a walk with our daughters when they were growing up. Even our seemingly ever present blisters were not overly troubling us. It was good to be alive.

We were walking again by 3 after a nice lunch in the company of distinctly Midlands' accents. I'd even managed to win £7 on the fruit machine and we knew it was only 6 miles or so to Kempsey. Carol had a text message from Alison, our elder daughter, to say that she had passed her driving test; it really was a red letter day! It took two hours or so to reach Kempsey but the Anchor hadn't opened yet. Not to worry, we drove back to Tewkesbury, stopping at a riverside pub for the drink we'd promised ourselves at the end of a lovely day. And I won another £8 on the fruit machine. By 7:30 we were back in Sutton Coldfield, tired but a little euphoric. We'd made it home, at least.

Day 17 Wednesday 17 May 2000 Kempsey to Kidderminster

Our next three legs, Kempsey to Kidderminster, Kidderminster to Wolverhampton and Wolverhampton to Stafford would be based from home. We waited at the same bus stop that we'd waited at on 26 April when we set out for Lands End. This time, we were catching a train to Worcester, from where we would make our way back to Kempsey. The weather was pretty much the same as on 26 April, damp, overcast and with the threat of rain in the air. However, the bulging rucksacks had gone to be replaced by just the one day sack, containing our waterproofs, the Phillip's Navigator road map and some water.

Although we missed the train we'd aimed for, we were still in Worcester by 9:30 and got a taxi back to the Anchor at Kempsey. It didn't take us too long to reach Worcester, a lovely city that I knew quite well from outings with friends to the races and cricket matches. We passed the Talbot Hotel, where I usually stopped when in Worcester, and soon found the A449 that we'd be pretty much following all the way to Stafford. By now, although it had warmed up somewhat, the threat of rain had materialised and we needed our waterproofs for the first time on our journey.

Thankfully, there were pavements all the way along the A449 and, although Carol was hampered by a particularly pernicious blister on her heel, we made pretty good progress until we neared Ombersley. Just short of the village, in a layby at a place called Hawford, we came across a memorial called the "Jardin de Celine". It marked the spot where the body of a French girl called Celine Figard had been found in 1995. She had accepted a lift from a lorry driver who subsequently raped and murdered her before dumping her body there. As parents of daughters of about the same age as Celine we found the site particularly poignant. Her murderer was sentenced to life and ordered to serve a minimum of 20 years in prison. It would be her parents and family who would serve the real life sentences, however.

A dual carriageway bypass took the A449 around the village but we were able to take the A4133 through the village centre. I've seen Ombersley described as picturesque, which it undoubtedly was. My word to describe the ambience we encountered would be snooty, however. This was epitomised by the gracelessness of the barmaid who took our lunch order at the Kings Arms. Perhaps we'd trodden in something on the way in? We'll never know but her attitude was appalling.

By 3pm we were back walking, soon re-joining the busy A449. We enjoyed good footpaths, although Carol was really suffering from her painful blister and we were both pretty worn out. Then, about three miles short of Kidderminster, the footpaths ran out. By now, the rain had intensified and the oncoming cars were travelling particularly quickly. It was the worst traffic we had encountered since setting out and for the first time I felt really apprehensive. Thankfully, we made it to Kidderminster Station without mishap and caught the 18:31 train back to Birmingham. We were wet, tired and dispirited and it later turned out that at 21.4 miles, we'd done our longest leg of the trip to date.

We were back home by 19:35, just in time for the UEFA Cup Final between Arsenal and Galatasaray of Turkey. It went to penalties and, as usual, the English side lost. What is it with English clubs and penalties? A wise man once told me that "Some days you're the pigeon, some days you're the statue". Today really had been a statue day for us.

Day 18 Thursday 18 May 2000 Kidderminster to Wolverhampton

Once again, we underestimated Birmingham's rush hour traffic and missed the train we were aiming for. No matter; trains were fairly frequent at that time in the morning and we were back in Kidderminster by 9:50, refreshed and ready once more for the fray. It was pouring with rain as we set out again on the A449. We were kitted out for wet weather, however, and made steady progress as we passed through Cookley and Stourton, pausing briefly for mugs of tea and kit-kat biscuits at one of the roadside snack bars that we'd grown to love in the same way that I imagine desert dwellers regarded oases.

We were soon in Staffordshire but were getting frustrated with the typically British weather. The frequent rain showers were followed by sunny spells which meant that we got over-heated in our rain wear and had to remove it. My left foot was hurting but we ploughed on until we reached Wall Heath, at the junction of the A449 and the A491, at 1:20. We lunched at the Wall Heath Tavern and I could not help but contrast the welcome we received there to that at the Kings Arms in Ombersley the day before. Give me a working class pub every time! As we read the papers over lunch we spotted that a man was into the 4th day of his challenging walk from Lands End to John O'Groats. Unlike us, he was walking backwards and planned to do the walk in 6 weeks, a shorter time than we had allowed. Good luck, I thought, you'll need it.

By 2:30 we were back walking, having ignored the friendly barman's advice that we should catch the bus. I reckoned that we had about six and a half miles to go and it was raining again but we had the joy of pavements for a couple of miles or so. Our luck ran out, however, and we once again faced yesterday's hazard of fast traffic, this time exacerbated by the rain. After nearly two hours or so we made it to the outskirts of Wolverhampton along the Penn Road. A welcoming café emerged from the gloom and we were served by a very nice man to mugs of tea and cakes.

At 4:45 we set out on the last mile and a half or so for the city centre, catching the metro that runs from Wolverhampton to Birmingham City centre along what once was an old railway track. Local knowledge meant that we knew that we could get off at West Bromwich and get a bus from there that went past our front door in Sutton Coldfield. We were home shortly after 7 after what had been a mixed day but grateful to be able to tick another day's destination off the itinerary. And as usual after a day on the road we slept like babies.

Day 19 Friday 19 May 2000 Wolverhampton to Stafford

Today's destination was Stafford, a town I knew quite well. In 1999 I had done some work for my brother Phil in the Crown Court there. Phil was a solicitor specialising in criminal work and based in London. He had a client facing trial for a drugs importation offence and rather than send someone up from London he asked if I would attend each day, sit behind the barristers and take a note. At that time I taken redundancy from my career with Birmingham City Council and was working part time four evenings a week for West Midlands Police so my days were free. The trial lasted 3 months, was absolutely fascinating and gave me the impetus to apply for my next full time job with an organisation dealing with miscarriages of justice. I got to know Stafford quite well during lunch breaks and lulls in proceedings and was looking forward to renewing my acquaintanceship with the town.

We reversed our homeward journey of the previous evening and were in Wolverhampton, via West Bromwich, by 9. Our route took us out of the city centre via Stafford Street and Stafford Road back to the A449. It was raining again and relatively cold compared to the last few days so we were glad to stop at a truck stop café after six miles or so for tea and bacon and sausage sandwiches. This coincided with a particularly heavy downpour, so we took our time and relaxed with the daily papers.

Half an hour later the rain had abated and we plodded steadily on for an hour and a half until we came to Penkridge. "The Railway" was our venue for lunch and again it was good to eat and drink in unpretentious surroundings. By 2:30 we were back walking and carried on non-stop to Stafford, arriving at the railway station at 4:40. My brother-in-law Bob was working in the area and had agreed to meet us there at 5:30 and give us a lift home as he only lived just around the corner from us. We had a cup of tea and a cake at the station cafe while we waited for Bob and reflected on the day. It had been rainy and cool but, if equipped for the weather, these were on balance better walking conditions. There had been pavements all the way, which was a real blessing after our experiences on the two previous days, and Carol's feet were feeling better. So our vote was definitely a "pigeon" day and we were quite happy as we relaxed in the back of Bob's car on the way home.

Day 20 Sunday 21 May 2000 Stafford to Newcastle-under-Lyme

We took Saturday 20 May off. Carol's beloved Aston Villa were playing Chelsea in the F A Cup Final and she wasn't going to miss that for the world. Not only did she want to watch the game, she wanted to be immersed in all the pre-match hype and entertainment. My allegiances lie with the Blue half of the City, so although I would watch the game, I wasn't bothered about the preliminaries. I took myself off to Sutton town centre and began browsing in the Clarks' shoe shop there. Somewhat belatedly I had realised that my feet were swelling as I walked for six hours or so each day and that it was the swelling that was causing my blisters. I found a range called "Cahill" that were an extra-wide fitting with cushioned insoles. They came in half sizes also and as soon as I tried a size 10 ½ I knew that these were the shoes for me; I had never felt so comfortable. Sold to the gentleman with a grin on his face! Sadly for Carol, the Villa lost 1-0 to Chelsea in what was, by all accounts, a pretty grim game but at least I had the satisfaction of a potential solution to my footwear problem.

So on Sunday, it was time for the cars again. We had used the Saturday to replenish our wardrobes and pack the car with the guides to the Northern half of England and Scotland that I had pre-ordered from Tourist Information Centres as we planned our trip. They were invaluable sources of accommodation and other local information as we processed northwards. I had booked us into the Durlston Guest House, just north of Newcastle-under-Lyme centre and we parked our cars there at 9:40. As we waited for Bob at Stafford Railway Station on the Friday evening I had seen that there was a bus service from Stafford to Newcastle and back. We walked into the town centre and caught the 10:10 bus to Stafford, thus ensuring that we would not have do any ferrying of cars on the evening.

By 11 a.m. we were back walking, this time along the A34 from Stafford. After four miles or so we stopped at The Greyhound Inn at Yarlet for a quick one then carried on until 1:30 when we stopped for lunch at the Walton Inn at Walton in Stone. This was one of the new style family pubs that had begun to proliferate and had a menu typical of that ilk but at least it opened on Sundays and wasn't over-priced. We were gone by 2:45 and walked for two hours, which is 6-7 miles at our usual pace, before stopping at the Poacher's Cottage at Trentham, another link in the chain of Harvester establishments but again thankfully open on Sundays. After an hour of relaxing and reading the Sunday papers we pressed on into Newcastle-under-Lyme. The town had an air of dilapidation about it. Like its bigger neighbour, Stoke-on-Trent, it seemed to be transitioning from manufacturing industries to service industries and not to be particularly enjoying the change.

We had a mile and a half to go to our guest house which we did in half an hour. My new shoes were performing magnificently but Carol was concerned at the size and structure of a particularly virulent blister that she had on her left heel. It was obvious that we needed to come up with a solution and we discussed the possibilities of medical attention and footwear changes as we chatted in bed that night. Knowing Carol as I did I was sure that she wouldn't let a blister defeat her having come so far, it was just a question of what to do for the best.

Day 21 Monday 22 May 2000 Newcastle-under-Lyme to Middlewich

We had an early (7:30) breakfast and chatted to our host, Mr Stott. He remembered that Noel Blackham had stayed at the Guest House and seemed interested in our acquaintanceship with him. We then drove in both cars to Middlewich and booked in at the Kinderton House Hotel. By 10:30 we'd driven back to Newcastle, parked up and were ready for whatever the day might bring.

Our route would take us via Alsager and Sandbach to Middlewich. On the way, we would pass from Staffordshire to Cheshire, which to my way of thinking counted as the North of England, albeit just. However, my friend Andy who is from Sunderland refers to anybody form anywhere south of Middlesbrough as a cockney! Whatever, the psychological boost we got from thinking we would have made it to the North was not to be denied.

We set out in cool and overcast conditions along the A34. Our first pit stop was for a cup of tea at one of our favourite road side cafes at 11:30. We carried on up the A34 before turning left on the A50 to Alsager. Although I had visited the town's college when playing basketball in the 1960's and early 70's I didn't recognise anywhere because our games were invariably played on dark winter nights. However, we soon tracked down the Lutley Arms and had a nice lunch at 1p.m.

Half a mile after the pub we turned left at Rode Heath, heading for Sandbach. By now, the showers of the morning had gone and it had become a lovely warm and sunny afternoon. Our road was the A533 and for 2 ½ miles there were no footpaths so we proceeded with caution along what really was a winding country road. Thankfully, we had paths for the last 1 ½ miles into Sandbach which turned out to be a pleasant little town. I had my hair cut at a barber's shop while Carol bought postcards which we sent on a pretty regular basis to update friends and family on our progress.

I reckoned that we had about 5 miles to go to Middlewich and had made good time so we stopped for a drink at the Fox Inn at Elworth after about 2 of those miles. Thereafter, the A533 road ran parallel to the Trent and Mersey Canal. This was a lot wider than the canals we were used to in the Midlands and, judging by the number of barges using it, was still used to transport goods. Possibly some of them were bound for the Bisto gravy factory, which we passed on our way, but I thought that a more likely candidate was salt from the British Salt Company that we then came to. Although I didn't know it at the time, Middlewich lies on the site of a pre-historic brine spring. Salt has been produced in the area since at least Roman times and the British Salt Company is still responsible for more than half of the table salt we use today.

It didn't take too long to get to the Kinderton House Hotel, which turned out to be one our better overnight locations. BBC North West was on the television so I was right; we were in the North of England! We had a leisurely drink and sandwich before heading back to Newcastle-under-Lyme to collect the second car. And as we drove, we resolved that we absolutely must do something to resolve the mother of all blisters on Carol's heel that had plagued her all day.

Day 22 Tuesday 23 May 2000 Middlewich to Northwich

We decided that we would have a short day today, stopping at lunchtime so that Carol could have her foot problem resolved. She had used the hotel's Yellow Pages directory to find a chiropodist in Northwich who could see her at 3 p.m. Northwich was about 7 miles away and we set out in one of the cars to check the location. We then used the local Tourist Information Centre to find accommodation for the night and booked in at the Ayrshire Guest House. We then returned to Middlewich happy in the knowledge that a solution was in sight for Carol and pleased to have a short day as not only was it raining but the forecast was that it would do so for the rest of the day.

Having accomplished our ferrying routine with the cars, we set out from our Middlewich hotel at noon. By 1:30, we were at the Bull's Head at Davenham having followed a nice, quiet road with footpaths all the way. This was a lovely pub and served great food. Tempting as it was to stay, we were underway again by 2:20 to walk the final mile and a half to the chiropodist who was located at Leftwich, just short of the centre of Nantwich. While Carol was attended to, I went around the Salt Museum, some 50 yards down the road. This gave a very interesting demonstration on the history of production of salt and also taught me that the suffix 'wich' originally meant a dwelling or hamlet but a special meaning 'salt-works', and found in the Domesday Book, developed; hence Middlewich, Northwich, Leftwich...

Carol joined me in the Museum café and we had tea and cake while she described her treatment. The chiropodist had lanced, drained and dressed what was a particularly deep blister, finally giving her dressings and ointment for the road ahead. I'm a bit squeamish about things like that but she took it all vey stoically and described feeling somewhat better already. Rather her than me!

As we walked on into Northwich we passed the headquarters of a company called Headwater Holidays. In 1998 and 1999 we had booked walking holidays with Headwater in France, firstly in the Dordogne region and secondly in the Franche-Comte region. These were absolutely great holidays; Company representatives met us off the train in France, took us to our first hotel and thereafter did more or less everything for us. The routine was that on day one we would set out on foot along sign marked Sentiers de Grandé Randonnée footpaths, unencumbered with baggage other than a day pack. The Company transferred our luggage to our next hotel, anything from 12-15 miles away, whilst we spent a leisurely day walking and lunching in a beautiful part of rural France. A typically delicious French dinner then awaited us and we enjoyed day two off to relax and explore the region before repeating the routine by setting out on foot for our next location on day three. And as a bonus, we tagged a three or four day stopover in Paris onto the end of one holiday. We also made some particularly good friends in Braidwood and Jim from Glasgow on the first holiday and had arranged to meet them as we broke our drive back from John O'Groats on the completion of our walk.

It didn't take long to reach our Guest House where we relaxed by watching 'Countdown', one of our favourite programmes and catching up on the news via the papers that we had stopped to buy. I took the opportunity to book our next two nights' accommodation before we drove back to Middlewich for car number two and filled up with petrol. By 8 we were back at the Guest House repaired, replenished and ready for whatever day 23 of our great adventure might have in store.

Day 23 Wednesday 24 May 2000 Northwich to Lowton

As we listened to Sarah Kennedy over breakfast she included in her traffic announcements that the A533 at Norwich was closed due to essential gas repairs. I'd been to Norfolk often enough to know that most of the roads in that county started with the number '1'. In addition, we planned to start our drive from Northwich to Lowton, our next overnight stop, via the A533 from Northwich. So I checked the teletext service on BBC and discovered that it was the road that we planned to use that was closed. Our trusty Phillip's Navigator soon came up with a diversion and we drove both cars to the Red Lion at Lowton, returning by the same route to Northwich.

At 10:45 we set out on foot via the most direct route, as was our usual policy, along the A533. Our reasoning was that it would be open to pedestrians who would not look favourably on a three or four mile diversion and we were quickly proved right. Soon we turned right on to a country lane heading for Anderton, then Comberbach. Our route took us along the canal through Marbury Country Park and we agreed that it was some of the nicest walking we'd done so far.

The Moorings Restaurant at Anderton Boat Marina provided a convenient spot for a drinks break and we spent some time chatting to the barman, who took a keen interest in what we were doing. Not long after leaving the restaurant, we had what I can only describe as a close encounter of the bovine kind. As we rounded a corner we could hear an almighty bellowing. Just ahead of us, a large beast was trying to clamber over a wooden fence. Now we are both very much city dwellers through and through and it was not immediately clear if this was a cow, a heifer, a bullock or, perish the thought, a bull. As we looked unsuccessfully for an escape route the weight and bulk of our potential nemesis brought the fence down and it was free! Luckily, it

60

turned out to very obviously be a cow and it calmly trotted through a gate to our right to be re-united with the rest of the herd. We gathered later that separation from the herd had caused its distress.

We passed through Comberbach before turning left at Gibb Hill on to the A559. This took us through Antrobus and on to the Ring O'Bells at Lower Stretton by 1:15. Very much to our chagrin, a sign outside said 'No Food Available Today'. However, it was pretty clear from our map that there was no prospect of reaching another pub before 2 p.m., the usual time for last food orders in country pubs. Determined to have a drink and sit down at least we went in. And, bless them, they had pork pies. Now I'm as susceptible to a pork pie as the next man and it went down a treat with a pint. Carol gladly joined me; after all, we were burning off the calories as we walked, weren't we? The locals were a very friendly bunch and all interested in what we were doing. Just before we went at 2:15, they had a whip round and presented us with a pound each for the Multiple Sclerosis Society. Would that have happened in snooty Ombersley? I don't think so.

Not long after leaving the pub we crossed the busy M56 at Junction 10 before joining the A49 bound for Warrington. The southern suburbs of the town were very pleasant and leafy and at Stockton Heath, we came across a Clarks' shoe shop. My Cahill extra wide fitting size 10 ½ shoes that I had bought when we stopped off at home had proved an absolute boon, so I decided to get some more just in case. Carol was also looking to get some of the same style but sadly we were out of luck; they didn't have our sizes in stock. Not long afterwards, we came to the Manchester Ship Canal. I had been impressed with the width of the Trent and Mersey Canal but this was something else. Opened in 1894 to link Manchester to the Irish Sea, the canal soon turned Manchester into Britain's third busiest port, even though it is 40 miles inland and 60 feet above sea level. As was our routine when we came to somewhere interesting, we got a passer-by to take our picture with the canal in the background.

We carried on along the A49, skirting the town centre of Warrington. The Northern suburbs were different from the Southern with a fair amount of commercial and industrial activity. At 4:15 we stopped at a McDonalds for coffee, a burger and a rest. We read the papers before re-joining the A49. At Winwick, we took the right hand fork along the A573, passing through Hermitage Green. This was a pleasant stretch with views of what could only be the Pennines on our right.

At Lowton, we took a right turn along the A572 for the last mile to the Red Lion. Food was still being served until 9:30 but we weren't hungry and relaxed by sampling the activity on the pub's crown green bowling green and watching the Champions League final between Real Madrid and Valencia. Much as we both love football, it was hard to get into a match between two Spanish teams so we went back to Northwich to collect our other car before retiring to reflect on what had been quite an eventful day.

Day 24 Thursday25 May 2000 Lowton to Charnock Richard

Considering that the Red Lion had served food the previous night until 9:30 our breakfast in the morning was nothing to write home about. Croissants, cereals and a flask of cold milk had been left outside our room overnight; perhaps chef only works in the evening? We drove to the Hunters Lodge Motel just north of Charnock Richard and left a car. As we arrived back at Lowton the heavens opened so we sat in the car until 10:30 when it abated somewhat then got underway.

The B5207 took us to the A537 where we turned right heading towards Wigan. We were at Platt Bridge by 12 and, having had no hot food at breakfast, gave in to the temptation of hot beef and onion barm cakes from Beaston Bakery which we ate with cups of tea al fresco on a bench outside the shop. Delicious. Re-invigorated, we set out once more on the A537 before we re-joined the A49, the road we'd walked for much of the previous afternoon, at Ince-in-Makerfield.

The road skirted the centre of Wigan, so we were not near the legendary pier, site of George Orwell's canal scene as depicted in his book' The Road to Wigan Pier'. The book deals mainly with the living conditions of England's working poor. I hope you'll forgive me if I re-print a small extract "I remember a winter afternoon in the dreadful environs of Wigan. All round was the lunar landscape of slag-heaps, and to the north, through the passes, as it were, between the mountains of slag, you could see the factory chimneys sending out their plumes of smoke. The canal path was a mixture of cinders and frozen mud, criss-crossed by the imprints of innumerable clogs, and all round, as far as the slag-heaps in the distance, stretched the 'flashes' — pools of stagnant water that had seeped into the hollows caused by the subsidence of ancient pits. It was horribly cold. The 'flashes' were covered with ice the colour of raw umber, the bargemen were muffled to the eyes in sacks, the lock gates wore beards of ice. It seemed a world from which vegetation had been banished; nothing existed except smoke, shale, ice, mud, ashes, and foul water".

Books like Orwell's and Robert Tressell's The Ragged Trousered Philanthropists were an inspiration to me in my rebellious youth and although I gather that the location of the pier has long since been transformed I would have liked to pause there and reflect on what life for the working classes must have been like only 60-70 years earlier. We pressed on, however, eventually pausing at the Touchline pub for half an hour's rest and relaxation. The pub had a sporting theme but was mainly devoted to rugby league, an alien game to most Midlanders but one very popular in the North West of England.

We had our second downpour of the day near Haigh Country Park just north of Wigan but thankfully managed to find shelter at a bus stop. The rest of the day's walking was in a more rural setting with views of the Pennines to our right and we arrived at The Hunters Lodge Motel at 5 after a relatively short day for us of just over 14 miles. We knew we had a longer day coming up tomorrow, however, so we took the opportunity to relax before going to collect our other car at 8.

Day 25 Friday 26 May 2000 Charnock Richard to Bilsborrow

We were underway on the A49 again at 10:30, having done our usual relay with the cars to Bilsborrow, our destination for the day. Our first coffee break was at a village called Euxton, quiet now but home to over 40,000 people in World War II, when it was the site of a munitions factory and reputedly the place where Barnes-Wallis' bouncing bombs, used in the famous Dambusters raid, were made.

As we made our way past Leyland heading towards Preston on what was now quite a humid morning we were rewarded with views of the unmistakeable Blackpool Tower on our left. I calculated later that night that it was 14 miles away. The B6258 took us off the busy A49 as we walked through Bamber Bridge and for the first time on our walk we were forced to give way to a train as we halted at the level crossing next to Bamber Bridge station. We then joined the A675, pausing for lunch at The Vineyard in Walton-le-Dale, just south of Preston city centre.

We took our time over what was a lovely lunch, using the opportunity to try and find accommodation for forthcoming nights. Lancaster, our scheduled Saturday stop, proved particularly difficult with all B&B venues fully booked for what was a bank holiday weekend. Eventually, I managed to get a room at the Royal Kings Arms Hotel (AA***, for what that's worth). This was pricy compared to what we usually paid but had parking and was in the centre of the city. I then rang Brendan and Sue, good friends of ours and former work colleagues. They had kindly invited us to stop a night at their home in Skipton on our way north. By my reckoning, we would be as near to them as we were going to be on Monday night and we agreed that we would drive to Skipton from wherever we finished walking that night.

As we left The Vineyard the morning's humidity had turned to rain; in fact it was pouring down. Undeterred, we ploughed on into Church Street in Preston city centre, looking for Clarks' shoes for Carol in particular. The relatively recent homogenisation of town and city centres as far as shops were concerned meant that we were pretty sure to find a Clarks shop and sure enough we did. Sadly, there was nothing suitable in Carol's size so we carried on down Church Street, pausing for a few things at the mandatory Boots shop that, like Clarks, you are pretty sure to find in a reasonably large town and certainly in a city.

A friendly postman gave us directions to the northward bound A6 and we pressed on, determined to get the last 7 miles or so under our belts as quickly as possible. Although the trainers Carol was wearing were comfortable, they were far from waterproof and her feet were soaking. By now, traffic was tailing back along the A6, presumably resulting from a combination of the rush hour and holiday makers heading for the Lake District and elsewhere for the Bank Holiday Weekend. A stationary car driver wound his window down to remark that it was quicker to be walking like us than driving. Soaked as we were, I mulled over whether or not I would swap places with him and, superficially attractive as the idea was, it would have been cheating, wouldn't it?

We got to Bilsborrow at 6:30 to discover one of the nicer B&B's that we'd stopped at. It was right on the Lancaster Canal and our room had a lovely view over it. Plus, there was a mini-bar! Temptations like that should not be put in the path of wet and weary walkers. I'm sure I resisted but can't recall now if it was for 5 or 10 minutes.

At 8, we went to get the other car, noticing as we went that there was a bus stop outside the B&B with a timetable for buses to Lancaster. That held out the prospect of a 'no relay' day. If only we could be guaranteed a 'no rain' day…

Day 26 Saturday 27 May 2000 Bilsborrow to Lancaster

Mrs Bolton, our hostess at Bilsborrow, gave us a bus timetable for the number 40 service to and from Lancaster. We drove there, parked in the carpark of the Royal Kings Arms Hotel, got the 10:13 bus back to Bilsborrow and were walking again by 11 a.m. Yesterday's rain had passed over and it was a lovely fresh day, not too hot and with a pleasant breeze; in fact perfect walking conditions. And as we proceeded up the A6 we saw, for the first time in our lives, a weasel or a stoat. I know that one is bigger than the other but as it was a solitary specimen we had nothing to judge it against. Up until now, the only out-of-the-ordinary examples of rural fauna that we'd seen had been badgers and they were inevitably dead by the roadside.

Just before Catterall we took the B6430 road. This looked more direct than the A6, which took a curve to the left at this point. It also held the promise of being a quieter road, something that always held an attraction for us. We stopped for coffee at the Wyreside Café, just short of Garstang, and sat overlooking a colony of sand martins toing and froing from their nests in the sandy banks of the River Wyre. A buzzard circled overhead and I thought how idyllic it was just to sit and watch nature in all its glory; far better than the hustle and bustle of city life that had been the background to my working environment for the last 30 something years.

After half an hour we were underway again, re-joining the A6 shortly after the small market town of Garstang. We stopped for lunch at the New Holly Inn at Forton but didn't linger; Carol wanted to get to Lancaster before the shops shut to look for some new trousers and we walked at a markedly quicker pace than usual. At frequent intervals solitary cyclists passed by, fully kitted out in Lycra and wearing numbers. I'd seen enough of the Tour de France to think that this couldn't be a race; competitors usually grouped together over the course of a race, taking turns at the front as the most energy efficient way of progressing. A sedentary marshal eventually explained that it was a ten mile time trial, open to three wheeler bikes as well as the usual bicycles and I thought how pleasant a way to spend an afternoon that would be.

We passed the University of Lancaster and entered the city via Scotforth Road and South Road at 4:45. I went straight to our hotel and Carol headed for the shops. She joined me after not too long, having had no luck looking for trousers but having bought sandwiches for our tea. We ate them pretty much in silence, feeling tired after what was not too long a day for us in terms of mileage but one where we'd walked more quickly than usual and had not stopped as often or for as long as usual. Moreover, we were disappointed with our room, which was small, cramped and very hot, so much so that we had to have the window open thereby letting in noise and fumes from the passing traffic in the busy city centre streets. Our only consolation was that we didn't have to fetch a car but on balance I would rather have done that and enjoyed a comfortable room somewhere else.

Day 27 Sunday 28 May 2000 Lancaster to Crooklands

In the morning, the hotel made amends to a small degree by laying on a good breakfast, including smoked haddock and poached egg for Carol. As we checked out, the receptionist asked if our room had been satisfactory. When Carol said we had been very disappointed with it, the receptionist reduced the bill by £10. We'll never know whether this was a spontaneous gesture of goodwill on her part or the result of previous complaints by dissatisfied guests but it helped a little. Our mood soon worsened, however, as we had to wait 20-30 minutes for a car that was blocking our way out of the car park to be moved.

We were eventually walking by 11:20, having left a car at the Crooklands Hotel, our next halt, and returned to Lancaster in the other. We exited the city via the Skerton Bridge over the River Lune, pausing shortly afterwards to have our photo taken with the picturesque Lancaster Castle in the background. Soon we were within half a mile of the sea at Bolton-le-Sands, as close as we'd been since setting out. Morecambe Bay was on our left and the hills of the Lake District ahead of us; those views and the unpolluted fresh air reminded us of one of the reasons we were doing our walk. We felt glad to be alive, out and about and enjoying some of the many delights that England has to offer for just a little effort on the part of the explorer.

The A6 took us inland once more towards Carnforth and by now the bank holiday traffic had turned it into a very busy road. The Carnforth Hotel provided us with a break and a very good Sunday lunch; delicious and two courses for just £4.95. We could not have been far from the town's railway station, the refreshment room of which was the location for the iconic final scene in David Lean's classic film 'Brief Encounter'. In 1999 it had been voted into 2nd place in a poll of the top 100 British films and the station still attracted fans from all over the world. Were we not otherwise engaged I've no doubt that we would have sought out the station, both being romantics at heart. We had done just that on holiday in Dingle, Ireland once, seeking out the isolated schoolroom location from another David Lean classic 'Ryan's Daughter' but we needed to press on and were underway again by 2:45.

After 2 miles, we took a right onto the A6070, a far quieter road, intrigued by the 'flood' warning sign that we saw as there had been no rain that day that we were aware of, although not long afterwards we came to what I can only describe as a large puddle which we managed to negotiate without mishap. We covered another 3 miles to Burton-in-Kendal. By now we were in Cumbria and celebrated by having a drink in the Kings Arms where a regular told me that there had been a very heavy downpour there at 1 p.m. So today, we had been pigeons rather than statues and kept dry by a matter of an hour or two.

We then had a fairly uneventful 3 miles or so along the A6070, passing a field of llamas as we walked. I know that worldwide these members of the camel family are farmed for meat, their wool and their hides but I'm not sure why they are becoming more and more popular in Britain. One particularly curious animal followed us down the field, popping its head over the fence every so often. Eventually we stopped and Carol took a picture of it with me, which seemed to be what it wanted. I suppose there's no accounting for taste!

At a traffic island, we took the A65 road for a mile or so and came to Crooklands at 6:15. Our hotel was on the right and, unlike the previous evening, we had a lovely spacious room. Our feet and legs were feeling good so we quickly went to Lancaster to collect the other car. As we unpacked on our return, Carol discovered that she had left her dressing gown at the Royal Kings Arms Hotel. We phoned them only to be told that we would have to ring again in the morning and speak to the Housekeeper. I rang Brendan at Skipton and said we'd aim to be there by 4:30 the next day as we were only doing a short walk as far as Kendal. We booked an alarm call for 7:15 and continental breakfasts, retiring not long afterwards to mull over a very pleasant day on the whole: legs and feet good, nice meals, no rain for us and interesting and varied scenery. What's not to like?

Day 28 Monday 29 May 2000 Crooklands to Kendal

By 9 we'd had our breakfasts and Carol phoned the Royal Kings Arms Hotel. Her dressing gown was a nice silk one in the design of the flag of Australia. Our daughter Alison brought it back for her when she visited there with her cousin and Carol was most relieved when the housekeeper said she had it. While I went back to Lancaster to collect it, Carol washed her hair. We then set out for Kendal but were stuck in bank holiday traffic for an eternity. There was a medieval fair, or 'fayre', as these things are inevitably called, taking place in the town centre. Eventually, we made it to the Duke of Cumberland pub just north of the town but it was 12:15 before we got back to Crooklands, having left a car in the car park at the pub in Kendal.

We set out walking straight away on the A65 in what was pleasantly warm weather, stopping after about 4 miles for a sandwich at the Punch Bowl pub at Barrows Green. As we carried on, we were rewarded with lovely views of Kendal and the Lakeland hills in front of us. Although not in the Lake District National Park the town is known as the 'Gateway to the Lakes' and is, as we had already discovered, very popular with tourists, especially on a warm bank holiday. We avoided the 'fayre' as we passed through Kendal, stopping instead at a factory outlet shop to look at shoes but found nothing suitable for us.

At 3:45 we arrived at the Duke of Cumberland pub. Carol took advantage of the pub's facilities to change in readiness for our trip to see Brendan and Sue. We drove back to Crooklands, swapped cars and set out along the A65 towards Skipton. Once again we got caught in traffic but at least the scenery compensated to a degree. I could understand why Sue had wanted to move back to where her roots were. Equally, I could understand Brendan not resisting overly much. He, like my dad, came from County Cork, another

73

picturesque part of the world. I'd first met him in the late 1960's when as work colleagues we'd studied for professional exams together under the tutelage of Finbar Hegarty, another Cork man. If the truth be told however, we spent most of the time nattering and eating Mrs Hegarty's cakes. I'd also got to meet up with him when we were on holiday once at his family home in Cork which was literally over the road from the house of one of my many Irish cousins.

We reached our destination at 5:15 and more or less straightaway, and to my eternal shame, Brendan, Carol and I adjourned to the Shepherd pub leaving Sue slaving over a hot Aga. Good soul that she is, she protested that she didn't mind and on our return had prepared a delicious meal for us. We then stopped up until midnight, which was late for us on our walk, catching up on news and putting the world to rights. It was a lovely ending to what had been, traffic apart, a most enjoyable day and we slept the sleep of the just, deservedly or not.

Day 29 Tuesday 30 May 2000 Kendal to Shap

Sue had to go to work this morning, so we said our goodbyes quite early. Brendan then cooked us a full English, or should that be full Irish, breakfast which we ate with relish. We knew that we had a challenging day today as we would be tackling the climb of Shap Fell, a legendarily difficult ascent amongst motorists when family cars had less in the way of horsepower and before the M6 motorway was built to the east of Shap. It also provided a challenge for trains in the days of steam engines, with extra engines from a nearby base being added to some trains to provide more oomph on the ascent. Whilst we could plough on at our own steady pace for a good part of the day on level ground we had never particularly enjoyed an incline, so it was good to load up on particularly tasty calories in readiness for the challenge that we would be facing.

We went back to Crooklands to collect our second car then drove to Shap, boking in at the Greyhound pub there, our destiny for the night. As we drove back to the Duke of Cumberland in Kendal via the route we would be walking we noticed that there weren't many potential re-fuelling stations on the way so it was good to spot the Plough Inn at about 5 miles north of our starting point and we made a mental note to get there for 2 p.m. Having parked up at the Duke of Cumberland, we had a quick drink there before setting off for Shap at 12:10 p.m.

It was very warm by now, the heavy downpour that we'd endured earlier whilst in the car having moved away to the east. At first the gradient wasn't too steep but as the warmth increased it seemed that the incline got proportionately steeper. By way of compensation, the views all round were a delight but it was still with a sense of relief that we came to the Plough at 1:55 p.m. What's more, the board outside said that meals were served from 12 to

2:30 seven days a week; bliss! Sadly, our delight was premature. The car park was deserted and all doors locked. We were gasping for a drink, having not stocked up at earlier opportunities in the expectation of a pub lunch. There was a bell on one of the doors with a 'B&B. sign underneath so I rang that. The young girl that answered said that her mom had gone out but she gave us both a glass of water and sold us some crisps. She also said that 'Kendal Caravans', which was 2 miles up the road had a café so we pressed on, somewhat refreshed but not in the way that we had been looking forward to.

It was turning out not to be our day. Kendal Caravans didn't have a café but a kindly soul in their reception office gave us both a glass of blackcurrant cordial and we chatted to him for 15 minutes or so about what we were doing and walking holidays that he had enjoyed in France. That short pause re-invigorated us and we pressed on, knowing that we had about 8 miles or so to go, mainly up hill and with no prospect of a refreshment stop. However, the views by now really were lovely and the ascent, although steep, was steady and in many ways preferable to the undulating hills of Devon that had sorely taxed us earlier in our walk.

We paused briefly at the summit of Shap and Carol took a picture of me next to a stone commemorating the efforts of those who had made possible what was described as 'an old and difficult route over Shap Fell before the advent of the M6 motorway'. As we began our more gradual descent we passed through road works controlled by traffic lights. This helped us in that we had spells of traffic-free walking followed by bursts of activity but at least they were pretty predictable. A heavy shower as we passed Shap Wells Hotel meant that we needed to put on our waterproofs but we knew that we only had two or three more miles to walk. And unbeknown to us, just a mile or so on our left was Sleddale Hall. This was the real life location of Uncle Monty's cottage in the 1987 cult film 'Withnail and I'. As such, it was a place of pilgrimage for the film's many fans and, just as at Carnforth two days earlier, I've no doubt that were we not pre-occupied we would have made the small diversion to see it. The film made it to a still laudable number 29 in the 1999 list of top British films as opposed to Brief Encounter's second place.

The sun re-appeared just as we got to the Greyhound Hotel at 6 p.m. After a quick cup of tea, we drove back the way we had walked, returning the same way, this time with consummate ease, and eventually relaxing with the day's papers as we had cod and chips in the hotel's restaurant. In our room later that evening I did a rough calculation and reckoned that we were now over half way to John O'Groats; surely nothing was going to stop us now?

Day 30 Wednesday 31 May 2000 Shap to Penrith

Our plan had always been to walk between 15-20 miles a day. However, we anticipated that we would have to be flexible on some days because of the possible difficulty in finding accommodation, particularly in the more sparsely populated parts of the country. This was one of those days. It was about 12 miles from Shap to Penrith so we looked for somewhere to stay between 3-8 miles north of Penrith. Our luck was out, however. The very few places that we found were full so we ended up booking in at Glen Cottage B&B in the town centre of Penrith. The accommodation was actually over an Italian restaurant and quite reasonably priced. On balance, the prospect of a relatively short day with an Italian meal afterwards was an attractive one and we left a car in a pay and display car park in the town. This was, I think, the first time we had had to pay to park but at £1.30 for the day we couldn't really complain.

After driving back to Shap we had a quick drink in the Greyhound Hotel and were back on the A6 at 12:20. The sun was out but the forecast promised showers in the afternoon. We were prepared for that eventuality, however. Traffic was fairly light, which was a relief because there wasn't much in the way of footpaths, and we were treated to views of the Pennines on our right and the mountains of Lakeland on our left. Not long afterwards a cyclist went past sporting a Lands End to John O'Groats T shirt. His pace was pretty sedate so I suspect that like us he wasn't out to break any records. And I also suspect that he, like us, would have liked to stop and chat. As was virtually always our practice, however, we were walking on the right hand side of the road facing oncoming, southwards bound traffic so it was not to be. I hope he made it; having done over half the distance I imagine it would have taken a lot to make him give up.

We stopped after about 5 miles at the Lowther Castle pub at Hackthorpe for a sandwich and a drink. By now, and despite being somebody who enjoyed a pint, I almost invariably drank shandy. It was far more refreshing after a couple of hours on the road. We were on our way again after half an hour or so, collecting a 107 bus timetable as we left. This was the route from Penrith to Shap and might be useful that evening to collect the car. We were walking parallel to the M6 for the next few miles and crossed that busy road at a couple of points. Just south of Penrith we stopped on a bridge over a small river for a look, something that I almost invariably do when I come to a river. As we chatted to a very nice lady, she told us that it was the River Lowther that would soon join the River Eamont. That in turn would join the River Eden which flowed through Carlisle not too far from the sea. Carlisle would be our next stop after Penrith. And after that, we would soon be in Scotland!

By 4:30, we were at our B&B but it was shut. We stopped off at the local Tourist Information Centre and picked up a timetable for the bus service from Penrith to Carlisle then went and had a cup of coffee. By then, the B&B was open and certainly looked good value for money with an en suite bathroom and bath. I caught the 17:45 bus to Shap to collect one car and Carol moved the other one from the car park to outside our accommodation as by now parking was free there. She also booked us into accommodation in Carlisle for two nights as we planned to have a day off there as we did every now and then to catch up on laundry, etc. At 7:30 we went downstairs for what was one of the more memorable meals on our trip, including free liqueurs, and were back upstairs at 9:30, just in time to take a call from Laura. We slept well that night.

Day 31 Thursday 1 June 2000 Penrith to Carlisle

We had breakfast at 7:30 today and by 8:30 were driving to Carlisle. We left the cars in a road at the side of the Abbey Guest House in London Road, which was to be our home for the next two nights, and caught the 104 bus back to Penrith. As we travelled Carol spotted a timetable for buses from Carlisle to Gretna Green, which was to be our destination after Carlisle. These local buses were proving invaluable, especially on longer days in that they saved us from driving back to our previous destination in the evening to collect a car.

The 104 dropped us right outside Glenn Cottage in Penrith and we were walking again by 10:45. We anticipated being on the A6 all day but the larger scale of the Phillips Navigator map came up with a small side road that was straighter than the A6 which took a curve not long after Penrith. This road probably saved us half a mile or so; every little helps! Again we were relatively high up and blessed with good views of the Cumbrian Fells on our left and the North Pennines on our right. Decent scenery always makes a walk more enjoyable and although the weather forecast had promised rain throughout the day all we'd had was a few odd spots; certainly nothing to complain about. At Plumpton, having re-joined the main road, we stopped at Calico Aquatics, home to many aquariums replete with exotic species and, thankfully for us, a café where we had coffee and biscuits before setting out on the A6 once more.

We had our leisurely lunch at the Baronswood Restaurant just before High Hesket, reading the daily papers as we dined. The proprietor told us that she had quite a few 'end-to-enders' stop there and we were later to discover that it was a good job that we did stop as there was nowhere else open between there and Carlisle, some 9 miles further on. Every other potential halt would be either closed or boarded up. City dwelling, with its ready access to pubs, cafes and restaurants, had spoilt us and we were having to learn to keep a look out for possible stops; this would be particularly important as we approached Scotland where, particularly in the North West, we would be travelling through very sparsely populated stretches.

At 3:30 we set forth on the A6 once more with a nice breeze for company. We also were accompanied for long stretches by oystercatchers, largish wading birds with a distinctive call that, being wading birds, we never saw in Birmingham but that would prove to be frequent companions near to the coast as we progressed north. Eventually we traversed the Golden Fleece Roundabout where the M6 and the A6 met at Junction 42. There was a large truck stop café there literally heaving with lorries but despite being thirsty we carried on towards Carlisle, eventually stopping at 6 pm at the Green Bank pub, knowing that we only had a mile and a half to go, or half an hour at our usual pace.

We finally reached the Abbey Guest House at 7:15, having stopped at a Co-operative shop for fruit and yoghurt for our tea. Somewhat incongruously there was a security guard on duty there which made us wonder what the locals were like. We'd both grown up on council estates in what would be called relatively less salubrious parts of Birmingham but hadn't come across guards in shops previously to the best of our recall. It was a relief not to have to go and collect a car as we were both feeling tired and looking forward to our imminent rest day. And by now the rain forecast for the day had arrived with a vengeance, so after taking a phone call from our elder daughter Alison we had an early night.

Day 32 Saturday 3 June 2000 Carlisle to Gretna Green

We had used our day off in Carlisle to full advantage, even though it had rained continuously throughout the day. Carol had her hair done; first things first! She then walked around the corner to the launderette whilst I booked accommodation for the next three nights at Gretna Green, Lockerbie and Moffatt respectively. Gretna proved particularly difficult, doubtless because the town was still a popular venue for weddings. I'm not sure why this remains the case; historically, Scottish marriage laws were less stringent than English ones and Gretna was the first town over the border. There isn't much difference in the two countries' laws nowadays, however, so presumably it's the historical and romantic connotations that attracts couples.

After lunch in Carlisle city centre, we did some shopping. Much to my delight, I found a pair of size 10 ½ Cahill shoes in the Clarks' shop, thus ensuring that footwear would not be a problem for me for the rest of the walk. Carol bought a couple of things and we rang her sister Norma to finalise arrangements for her and her husband Bob, our Good Samaritan at Stafford, to collect our daughter Laura from Swansea University at the weekend. Finally, we collected bus timetables that showed we could use public transport between Gretna, Lockerbie and Moffatt, thus avoiding shuttling the cars for three days.

So by 10:30 today we were back at our previous finishing point in Carlisle, having caught the 382 bus service back from Gretna. For the first time on our trip, we would have to make a fairly big detour today. The direct route for us would be via the A74 but we knew from Noel Blackham's book that this was virtually a motorway, linking as it does the M6 and the A74(M), the main road from England to Glasgow. Theoretically, I suppose, we could have walked down it as Noel did but he found it an absolute ordeal and traffic would only have worsened in the intervening years. So we opted for the far quieter, but far safer, A7 and A6071, a dogleg that added about three miles to the journey. And, of course, we were only doing a short day today.

We paused briefly at Carlisle Castle for a photo call then crossed the River Eden before passing through Stanwick. At Kingstown, some 2 ½ miles further on, we stopped at a McDonalds for coffee before negotiating the traffic island at Junction 44 of the M6, the meeting place of that motorway and the A74. One glance at the volume of traffic, particularly the number of heavy goods lorries, told us that we had made the right decision about our diversion. And as we paused briefly on the A7, we were joined by an audience of inquisitive cows, something that I doubt would have happened on the direct route. Having said that, our chosen road was still relatively busy as it links Carlisle to Edinburgh and there were no footpaths for at least four miles of it.

Our lunch was taken at 12:30 in the Lyneside Café at Westlinton, next to the River Lyne. As usual, we took our time, talking at length to the proprietor. He said that he got quite a few 'end-to-enders' stopping there and guessed that was what we were doing. We were gone by 2 pm, passing through Longtown then crossing the River Esk before taking a left turn along the AA6071. Longtown, with its thriving cattle market, reminded me very much of Kanturk, my father's hometown in the Republic of Ireland and provided a good illustration of the very varied architecture and lifestyles that we had come across on our travels. It was also the site of a very large and heavily guarded defence munitions store which we passed. Apparently, it was the presence of nearby munitions factories that led the wartime Government of the day in 1916 to nationalise the brewing, distribution and sale of liquor in an area centred on Carlisle, the purpose being, entirely understandably I suppose, to control drunkenness amongst the munitions workers. Buying 'rounds' of drinks was forbidden! The scheme was still in operation in the 1960's and to experience it was the prime reason that I interrupted a hitch hiking trip to Edinburgh in about 1967 to spend a night in Carlisle. My recollection was that a pint of beer was one old penny cheaper than at home in Birmingham but that the beer itself was nothing special. And, in accordance with the old law, nobody bought me a pint.

After an hour or so, we crossed the River Sark, just before Gretna. I hadn't heard of this river previously but the adjacent 'Welcome to Scotland' sign confirmed that it formed the border between England and Scotland at this point. Of course, we stopped for the obligatory picture but more so to take in what was for us not so much in the way of a physical landmark but absolutely a very big psychological point in our journey. We had walked the length of England!

Gretna Green is actually a small village slightly to the north of the town of Gretna. It was very much as we expected, totally dominated by the wedding 'industry'. We paused to take in a couple of weddings, one accompanied by a piper. We bought postcards, which we wrote in a bar whilst we had a drink and a snack, then posted them in a 'special' post box in a gift shop next to the legendary blacksmith's shop. We asked a passing Dutchman to take our picture, which he did, wishing us a happy life together. I didn't like to disillusion him. There was a general air of happiness and celebration about the village and I began to see what the attraction was. And after all, it would be far cheaper than flying to that other popular wedding destination, Las Vegas.

By 6 pm we were at our guest house, Rhone Villa, which was only about 200 yards from the blacksmith's shop. It was quite cold by now and although the day had been cool, we had not had to endure any rain, unlike yesterday in Carlisle. I took the opportunity to book accommodation for Abington, our stop after Moffatt and we spent a pleasant evening reflecting on what had been not only an interesting day but a landmark one as far as our walk was concerned. All we had to do now was walk the length of Scotland.

Day 33 Sunday 4 June 2000 Gretna Green to Lockerbie

Today, entirely coincidentally, we would be walking between the sites of two of the biggest transport disasters ever to occur in Britain. In May 1915 at Quintinshill on the Glasgow to Carlisle railway just north of Gretna Green over 200 people, most of them soldiers on their way to Gallipoli, died in what remains the worst ever train crash in Britain. Then at Lockerbie in December 1988 a terrorist bomb brought down Pan Am flight 103, killing all 259 people on board and 11 people in the town. The Lockerbie incident, being only 12 years earlier, was still particularly fresh in our minds and we set out this morning very mindful that we would soon be arriving at a town whose name still resonated in the minds of virtually all British adults.

We were underway by 10:45 on what was a damp but breezy morning, having left both cars at Lockerbie and caught the 10:25 bus back to Gretna Green. Our road all the way to Lockerbie would be the B7076 which ran parallel to the A74(M) but would only, we were sure, be used by local traffic so held the promise of a quiet day. After an hour or so we came to an inviting café in a place called Kirkpatrick Fleming. Sadly, and in what would be an omen for the day, it was closed on Sundays. We pressed on, only pausing to chat to a one legged man in a wheelchair who was doing the end-to-end trip in the opposite direction in aid of the Firemen's Benevolent Trust. He had the help of a support team and after having our photo taken with him and making a donation we wished him well and set off again. An hour or so later we saw a sign for a pub advertising bar meals so took a slight detour to a place called Kirtlebridge, only to find that it didn't open until 7 pm on Sundays. Shucks! Or words to that effect. We found a nearby bench, always a boon to long distance walkers, and sat down to rest and regroup our thoughts. The only potential refreshment stop between here and Lockerbie would be at the town of Ecclefechan, so we decided to head for there, even though it would mean another slight detour.

By 2:15 we had reached Ecclefechan, birthplace of Thomas Carlyle, philosopher, historian and author, or so the sign said. A hotel on our left sported a sign saying 'Bar Meals 12-2 pm', we were too late! We then came to Carlyle's birthplace and enquired if there was a café or refreshments; no! Our last chance was the Ecclefechan Hotel, a pub that was not only open but advertised that it had food available. In we went and, true to form, there was no food, not unless you count three flavours of crisps, cheese and onion, spring onion or chip shop curry, hardly the epicure's ideal. Oh, and there were some out–of-date peanuts. Spoilt for choice, we opted for cheese and onion crisps (Carol) and stale peanuts (me). And there was no draught lager, my drink of choice for thirty years or so. I can't remember what I ended up drinking but we soon realised that the 'food' and drink were not the only issues; virtually every customer was foul-mouthed and drunk. In that regard, they were only outdone by the landlord. We beat a hasty retreat as soon as we'd finished our banquet. I later found out that Carlyle was, like his father before him, an irascible old goat. And he was particularly rude about my all-time hero, Charles Darwin. Perhaps there's something in the water in those parts that gets people agitated?

We arrived at Lockerbie at 5 pm, chilled (a cold wind had gotten up), tired and hungry. On the High Street we came across the Rendezvous Café, an absolute oasis. Not only was it open until 8, it served great fish and chips (me) and a jacket potato with chicken tikka (Carol). And we had a glass of wine each; we were back in civilisation. By 6:30 we were in the comfortable lounge in Tarras Guest House. Mrs Plaistow, our hostess, made us a cup of tea and we watched her very large television for a couple of hours. Carol spotted an Aston Villa video in the bookcase; apparently Mrs Plaistow's son was at a boarding school in our part of the world and shared Carol's enthusiasm for the Villa. Thankfully, for me anyhow, we were getting tired and didn't watch the video, retiring upstairs for showers and to a very welcome bed.

Day 34 Monday 6 June 2000 Lockerbie to Moffat

We spent a fair bit of time over our breakfasts this morning talking to a Forestry Commission employee, Adele Beck. Although originally from Gloucester, Adele was now based in Fort Augustus, the town where the Caledonian Canal ran into Loch Ness. We told her that, all being well, we would be passing through there in about 10 days' time and she invited us to pop in and see her for a cup of coffee. She also described the new Great Glen Cycleway that was adjacent to the main road and ran from Fort William to Inverness. Had we time to research that option it seemed superficially attractive to spend some time off the road but it wasn't clear how feasible it was and we opted to stay on the roads when we eventually reached Fort William. In any event, experience of holidays in Scotland had taught us that the plague of Scotland, *Culicoides impunctatus,* or the Highland Midge, to give it its English name, was more active in woodland areas and also that I seemed particularly attractive to the little pests.

By 8:30 we had set out to drive to Moffat. Once there, we had time for a cup of coffee before catching our bus back to Lockerbie and also to stock up on sandwiches, drinks, etc. for lunch. Our lesson from yesterday had not gone unlearnt. The 10:10 bus from Moffat got us back to our finishing point in Lockerbie for 11 o'clock and we set off straightaway on the B7076. On the bus down, we spotted a promising looking café at Dinwoodiegreen, about 7 miles north of Lockerbie and made a mental note to stop there. We reached the cafe after two hours of pleasant walking to be welcomed by a sign saying 'Closed on Mondays and Tuesdays until Further Notice'. But this time, unlike yesterday, we were prepared for that eventuality and had something to eat and drink before tackling the last ten miles or so into Moffat via a quiet country lane that our Navigator Atlas had revealed to us.

The next ten miles or so were probably as uneventful as any section of our walk to date. The weather was cool but not too breezy. There was virtually no traffic and little sign of habitation. Cattle seemed to be the main farming commodity and, for the second time on our travels, we saw a cow jump over a fence, this time sufficiently far away not to concern us. A lone cyclist, complete with panniers on his bike, passed us heading north and we speculated that he could be doing the same trip as us. We had sandwiches and a drink sat on a bridge over the Coomb Burn before proceeding on our leisurely way to Moffat. About a mile from the town we crossed the Southern Upland Way, a long distance foot-path of some 212 miles running from east to west across Scotland. Just after that, I had a phone call from my new employers confirming the start date for my new job as 10 July 2000.

We were at our B&B by 5pm and decided to drive into Moffat for some tea. The spa town was very pleasant and boasted, at just 20 feet wide, the narrowest hotel in the world, called 'The Star Hotel'. We took the obligatory picture and also paused to admire a statue called 'The Moffat Ram' in the market place, commemorating Moffat's historical past as a centre for the wool trade.

We went back to our B&B at 6 and settled into what was a lovely room with delightful views. I booked some accommodation in Lesmahagow, our destination in two days' time. A little earlier in the day we had taken a call from our daughter Laura confirming that her flight to the USA, where she would be working for the summer, would be on 30 June 2000. As it would be inconceivable for us not to see her before she went and she would be relying on Dad's Taxis to get her to Gatwick Airport, our agenda was clear; we had to finish our walk by 27 June to allow 2 days to get back to Birmingham. We would have to plan accordingly and we turned our minds to that prospect, which we decided was achievable, before turning in for the night.

Day 35 Tuesday 6 June 2000 Moffat to Abington

Today's destination was Abington, just over 20 miles from Moffat. However, the only accommodation we were able to find was at Netherton Farm, 2 ½ miles north of Abington. Although it was on our route, we decided that a total distance of 23 miles to the farm in rain that was forecast for most of the day would be unduly taxing; in any event, our calculations on the night before had shown that by maintaining more or less our present pace we would get to our final destination, John O'Groats, by 26 June, i.e., with a day to spare. So we set out for Abington after loading up on full breakfasts that we had asked for in the knowledge that, as yesterday, there would not be many re-fuelling opportunities on the roads we would be walking.

By 10:45 we were back at our previous evening's finishing point, having left a car in a car park in Abington. The journey back had shown that the only possible stop was at Crawford, just 3 miles short of Abington, so we repeated yesterday's ploy of stocking up on food and drink from a shop in Moffat town centre to keep us going throughout the day. We also had cups of tea and cake in a coffee house before somewhat reluctantly leaving the warmth to join the A701 and a gentle ascent with lovely views which even the persistent rain and cold could not mar for us. After two miles, we took a slight left onto the B719. We were now quite high up and able to fully appreciate the beauty of the surrounding countryside; there were hills in every direction. We had another mile of ascending before starting our longish descent down what our Phillip's Atlas described as Greenhillstairs. Well, it was green and a hill but there were no stairs and we paused half way down for drinks and a sandwich which we enjoyed, despite the rain, sat on a convenient length of Armco safety barrier.

The 'stairs' eventually led us onto the A702 which would take us to Abington, running parallel as it did to the busy M74 and occasionally crossing the motorway. The main west coast railway line from London to Scotland also occupied the same territory and it wasn't long before all three routes crested Beattock Summit, immortalised in W H Auden's poem about a travelling Post Office 'Night Mail'. A signpost gave the height of the summit as 1016 feet but the ascent seemed gentler to us than that of Shap a week earlier. Not long afterwards we stopped again, taking advantage of the Armco barrier once more for something to eat and drink.

At 4:30 we arrived at Crawford, which seemed to consist of a single street about a mile long occupied by houses, three truck stops that were very popular with lorries leaving the M74 at the nearby Junction 14 and a pub, the 'Tudor House Hotel'. We opted for the latter and had a drink and some nuts. True to form, food would not be served until 6 p.m. but by now we were used to the vagaries of Scottish country pubs and our earlier shopping expedition in Moffat meant that we were not unduly inconvenienced. After half an hour, we were on our way again to cover the last three miles to Abington, arriving there at 6 p.m. By now the sun had finally made an appearance and as we drove back to Moffat to collect our second car we were able to fully appreciate the beauty of the area that we had spent the day in.

We received a very warm welcome from Mrs Hyslop at Netherton Farm and both agreed that it was the most impressive accommodation that we had come across to date. It had once been a hunting lodge for King Edward VII but now served as the house for a farm with a stock of some 120 beef cattle and some 1000 or so sheep. The royal connection was now maintained by Princes William and Harry who went shooting sometimes at nearby Crawfordjohn. She also told us that Sir Alec Douglas-Home, erstwhile, albeit briefly, British Prime Minister in the 1960's had owned a lot of land in the neighbourhood. She seemed particularly impressed with what we were doing. We, in turn, were delighted with our room and next door bathroom which were both beautifully appointed and we had a lovely night's sleep, the cold and rain of the day long since forgotten.

Day 36 Wednesday 7 June 2000 Abington to Lesmahagow

We were back walking on the B7078 by 10:10 today, having left a car at our overnight destination in Lesmahagow and driven the other one back to Abington. The weather was ideal for walking; bright, breezy and not too cold, which was just as well because our drive to and from Abington had revealed only two potential pit stops, a hotel not too far past Netherton Farm and Happendon Services which were about ten miles from Abington. It took us just under an hour and a half to reach the first option, The Red Moss Hotel, passing the entrance to Netherton Farm as we walked. And, as so many before it had been, it was closed. A sign outside promised that it would be open by 12 but we decided to press on, expecting to get to Happendon in about another hour and a half or so.

Just as on the two previous days our road was quiet with little sign of habitation and not much in the way of traffic. We were able to maintain a good pace, only stopping briefly for ten minutes or so to rest on a convenient grassy bank. There was a lovely flat cycle lane at the side of the road which we took advantage of and our spirits were lifted by the hills on either side of us. I'm always happy walking amongst hills, just as long as I haven't got to climb too many of them.

At 1:30 we arrived at Happendon Services, weary and ready for a break. We had a leisurely lunch, taking time to read the daily papers and ringing Laura to catch up on news from home. By 3 p.m. we were back walking again, knowing that we had just under six miles to go which would take us less than two hours at our normal pace. Our road was again quiet but, unlike this morning, we now had the busy M74 for company as the two roads were just yards apart all the way to Lesmahagow. At 3:50 we passed the Star Inn, not through choice as we'd have loved a drink but it was closed until 5:30. By

4:45 we had reached Lesmahagow, passing through the small town as our accommodation for the night, Kerse Farm, was about half a mile north of it.

Spots of rain had begun to fall as we turned in to the drive that led to the farm. There was woodland on either side and the area was very popular with dog walkers. Suddenly, a golden labrador that was off its lead ran at us. Its intentions were clear and it soon had a grip of my arm. I had been using a walking pole as an aide for some time but at that point Carol had it. Had she not, I would have used the pointed end to fend it off but it was not to be. The lady owner finally got the dog under control and was apologetic but suggested that it had gone for me because I'd had my hands in my pockets! Needless to say, that did not go down well with me and I remonstrated with her at some length. What if it had been a young child that had been attacked?

I'd calmed down by the time we reached our B&B at 5:10. We took our bags from our car leaving them in our room before driving back to Abington. On the way back, we stopped at the Star Inn, which was now open, and had a lovely meal of soup and beef stir fry. By 7:15 we were back at Kerse Farm. Mrs Hamilton, our hostess, was absolutely lovely and gave us tea and home-made cake. She also solved a problem that had been troubling us for some time; what to do for accommodation the following night. We had planned on stopping at Cambuslang but try as I might I could not come up with a B &B in the area. Mrs Hamilton suggested that we stop with her for another night and she would pick us up from wherever we finished walking. We didn't take much persuading, if any, and were soon settled in again what was lovely accommodation happy in the knowledge that the next day was taken care of.

Day 37 Thursday 8 June 2000 Lesmahagow to Dalmarnock

We set out this morning at 9:10, determined to take advantage of the early start made possible by the lack of necessity to shuttle cars and to walk as far as we could, hopefully past Cambuslang and into the City of Glasgow itself. That would be another psychological boost for us as the two biggest cities we would have to pass through, Birmingham and Glasgow, mark almost exactly the one third and two thirds distance points respectively on our journey. By tonight, all being well, we would have walked twice as far as the distance remaining to John O'Groats.

A fine rain, which was to last virtually all day, was falling as we set out, so full waterproofs were the order of the day. The Scots have a word for this sort of weather; dreek. And the word is onomatopoeic, i.e. one of those that sound exactly as it means. The B7078 provided us with footpaths for the first couple of miles or so and the traffic wasn't too heavy but every time a lorry went past we had to turn our backs to avoid the spray thrown up by its wheels. Soon we crossed the M74 at Blackwood, walking parallel to the motorway until we came to junction 8. By 11:45 we were passing through Machan and Larkhall, both showing the signs of dereliction that can befall industrial towns that have fallen on hard times as the local industries fell into decline. We stopped at a café for tea and a toasted sandwich before venturing out into the rain once more, heading for Hamilton, the next town of any size on our route.

Hamilton seemed more prosperous that the towns we had already passed through and it had the usual complement of shops that you find in large towns: Boots, Marks and Spencers, British Home Stores, etc. We found a decent pub on the north side of the town and put our feet up for half an hour or so before heading north-west once more on what was now the A724. Blantyre was the next landmark, birthplace of the explorer and missionary David Livingstone.

In 1877, 207 miners, both men and boys, were killed in an explosion in a coal mine there caused by methane gas, safety regulations having been disregarded in the interests of profit. As ever, the lives of the working class held little value for the employers.

We reached Cambuslang at 4:30 and it soon became clear why I had struggled to find accommodation hereabouts. The town had been, like many in South Lanarkshire, a centre for coal mining and iron and steel production. As those industries declined so, inevitably, did the town and it now had that air of dilapidation so common in former centres of heavy industry throughout Britain, including our own West Midlands. For some reason, I was expecting Cambuslang to be something of a rural delight. The name seemed to have a resonance about it. Perhaps I was subconsciously confusing it with Camusfeàrna, Gavin Maxwell's home in his autobiographical book 'Ring of Bright Water' and set in idyllic surroundings overlooking the Isle of Skye? Sadly, it was not a delight and after cups of tea and beans on toast in a café in the Town Centre we decided to press on to Dalmarnock, just north of the River Clyde and well and truly in the City of Glasgow.

There was a train station at Dalmarnock, which we reached at 6 p.m. The timetables showed a frequent service to Hamilton, which seemed to be the nearest station to Lesmahagow, so we rang Mrs Hamilton who kindly agreed to meet us there off the 6:15 train. It was a delight to see her friendly face and we relaxed in her car on our way back to Kerse farm after what transpired to be, at 23.3 miles, our longest day's walk to date. We spent some time that evening talking to Mrs Hamilton. She was very interested in our walk and had tackled the West Highland Way twice. I knew the Way started just to the north of Glasgow and that we would be crossing its path more than once as we progressed. She also explained that Kerse Farm was not a working farm and that the large bungalow she occupied was built to her and her husband's design. Like the vast majority of landlords and landladies that we had encountered she was kind, pleasant and helpful and we eventually retired looking forward to what we knew would be another very comfortable night. We were not disappointed.

Day 38 Friday 9 June 2000 Dalmarnock to Dumbarton

As we had our breakfast this morning Mrs Hamilton's dog started barking; a deer was running through the back garden. That was something we'd never come across in Birmingham! We were gone by 9 a.m., having promised Mrs Hamilton that we would send her a postcard from John O'Groats, so we were committed to finishing now.

Our drive to Dumbarton took us down three motorways and the A82 before we found our B&B for the night, as ever, uphill from the road. We left the cars there, having put a note through the door explaining that we would be back by about 8 on the evening. We then walked back to the A82 and caught a bus to Glasgow Central Station, passing the then Prime Minister Tony Blair in a small cavalcade as we proceeded. From the Station, we caught a train to Dalmarnock, finally resuming our walk at 12 o'clock, which was late for us.

Not long after leaving Dalmarnock Station, we passed Celtic Park, or 'Parkhead' as the fans call it, home to Celtic Football Club. We progressed via London Road to Argyle Street, ending up back at Glasgow Central Station. By now we were ready for lunch and found a little Italian restaurant, La Lanterna, in Hope Street just around the corner from the station. In our usual fashion, we took our time over lunch, celebrating reaching the two thirds distance with a nice bottle of red wine. We were gone by 2:30 and, whether it was the wine or not, for the first time in 600 miles we got lost. After half an hour of circuitous wandering, mainly attempting to avoid the Clydeside Expressway, we finally got a friendly lollipop lady to confirm that we had found the Dumbarton Road. She added that Dumbarton was an awfully long way to walk and let out a screech when we told her where we had come from and where we were going.

At 3:30 we came to a sign saying that we had eleven miles to go to Dumbarton, so we put our heads down realising that we had a long shift to do this afternoon. At Partick, we paused to make a couple of phone calls. I rang my brother Philip, a solicitor in London, to update him on our progress. All being well, he would join us in Wick on our last day and walk with us to John O'Groats. Carol then rang Laura to talk about her trip to the USA. We pressed on through Scotstoun and Clydebank before finally pausing at 6:30 in the shadow of the magnificent Erskine Bridge for a drink in a bar at Old Kilpatrick. We now had 4 ½ miles to go so limited ourselves to half an hour's rest, then proceeding through Milton before arriving at Dumbarton at 8:15. And we got some reward for the final uphill trek to our B&B because there was a beautiful view over the River Clyde to Dumbarton Rock and Castle from our room.

Day 39 Saturday 10 June 2000 Dumbarton to Inverbeg

Today, rather than getting a favour from our host we were able to provide one. Mr Muirhead, the gentleman in question, needed to get to Balloch to collect his daughter's car. She had been out the night before and had caught a taxi home to Dumbarton rather than drive after, presumably, a good night out. This wasn't a problem as we would be passing through where he wanted to go on our way to Inverbeg, which is on the shores of Loch Lomond. Favour accomplished, we carried on to our B&B at Inverbeg, encountering for the first time the dreaded *Culicoides impunctatus* that I mentioned earlier as we left a car at the Corries Guest House at Inverbeg. I'm guessing that it was the location of the accommodation, slightly uphill form the shore and in a woody area, which attracted the midges, but I resolved to stock up on repellent once back in Dumbarton.

By 10:30 we were off again on the A82, having acquired a supply of midge repellent. We took the A813 at Townend then passed through Bonhill before stopping for lunch at the Argyle Bar in Alexandria. Here we rang around, trying to find accommodation at Ardlui or Inverarnan, possible destinations for tomorrow, but without success. Luckily, Mrs Carruthers at the Corries at Inverbeg had a vacancy so we booked another night there. The landlady at the Argyle Bar was interested in what we were doing and told us that she had been to Lands End but not to John O'Groats. She also thought that Glasgow was 'rough' but I thought it politic not to comment.

After a very nice lunch we set off to Balloch and from there to Loch Lomond, taking advantage of a nice, quiet road that Mr Muirhead had shown us and eventually arriving at Duck Bay, a lovely spot with a marina and picnic area. It was good walking weather, sunny but not too hot and with a nice breeze. Fortuitously, there was a footpath at the side of the busy A82 and we were able to maintain a good pace, eventually arriving at Loch Lomond Golf Club. It's hard to imagine a better setting for a game of golf and the course was in a superb condition.

As we reached, from our point of view, the end of the golf course we saw a 'Public Footpath' sign that suggested that it might lead to a quiet road that ran parallel to the A82, eventually terminating at a spot called Luss. A Club official confirmed that this was the case and we walked for an hour in beautiful surroundings just yards from the loch side. We took a photo of what was, we thought, an unusual deer in that it was albino but my natural history knowledge did not extend to being able to say what species of deer it was. By now we had walked about 11 miles since lunch and were glad to stop at the 'Glendarroch' Tea Rooms for a cup of tea and something to eat. The establishment was named after the fictitious village in a Scottish soap opera called 'Take The High Road' as external shots were filmed in the village of Luss. It was easy to see why; there were beautiful views of Loch Lomond and its many islands and the surrounding mountains and forests.

After an hour or so we exited into what was by now heavy rain and re-joined the A82. We were able to stick to the footpath, for which we were most grateful as walking into heavy traffic in wet weather was not a pleasant experience as we knew only too well. We reached the Corries Guest House at 6:45 p.m., tired but having, we felt, enjoyed the best scenery of our walk to date. By 8 p.m. we had fetched the other car and were back in a lovely room with superb views over Loch Lomond. All we needed to do on the night was book accommodation in Tyndrum on Monday; that done, we were able to relax and look forward to tomorrow.

Day 40 Sunday 11 June 2000 Inverbeg to Inverarnan

Over breakfast we talked to two interesting couples. The younger one were on their way to Glencoe following the man's recent gap year tour around Australia. They seemed highly impressed with what we were doing. The older couple were from a place called Pemberton in South West Australia and had sold their vineyard to finance their trip to the United Kingdom. They were on their way to Uist in the Outer Hebrides via Skye. Apparently, it had been a fishing haunt of his when he was younger. He also said that an ancestor of his had walked from John O'Groats to Lands End in the late 19th century and had written a book about his trip which, although never published, was still in the family. Now that would be a fascinating read for us…

By 10:15 we were walking again, albeit with a sense of apprehension. Noel Blackham had described the next section as scary, with a long section of the A82 after Tarbet being single carriageway, twisting and winding, with no footpaths and occupying virtually all the land between the steep rock face that would be on our left and Loch Lomond on our right. Our drive back from Inverarnan, where we had parked our lead car, confirmed Noel's assessment and we knew that we would have to be at our most vigilant over the course of that section. In the meantime, however, we soon found ourselves, via a footpath, on what Mrs Carruthers at the Corries recommended and described as the 'old' road. This was what obviously served the area before the newer A82 was constructed. Although it was complete with old style cats' eyes and road markings, there was no traffic. Picnic tables had been set up at intervals and there were stunning views all the way down the Loch. We passed one other couple out walking but other than that the only signs of habitation were two cottages that we walked past. This was heaven!

Sadly, all good things have to end and we re-joined the busy A82 about a mile before Tarbet. At Tarbet, the road forked, the A83 taking a fair share of the traffic as it turned to the left on its way to Campbeltown via Lochgilphead. We stayed on the A82 and were about to enter the section that had given us such a sense of foreboding in the morning. To add to our worries, it started raining so it was a relief when, after 1 ½ miles, we came to a weaving centre with a coffee shop and were able to stop for lunch. We were gone by 1:15 and, thankfully, the rain had stopped. The next six miles were the ones we had been dreading but we had no alternative but to plough on, facing the oncoming traffic in the main. Two factors helped; the road was so twisting that cars could not attain high speeds and the traffic was coming in spurts. This, we later found out, was because traffic lights controlled a particularly narrow section of the road and limited movement to one direction. On occasions, all we could do was stand to the side of the road and allow the traffic to pass before making progress in the intervening lulls.

At 3:50, we arrived at Ardlui which marked the northern end of Loch Lomond. The little hamlet had a railway station and a busy marina and was, obviously, a popular tourist destination. We stopped for a drink at the Ardlui Hotel, glad to get out of the rain that had started once more and also pleased to have negotiated a particularly difficult stretch of the route. We knew that the last mile and a half to Inverarnan was served by a wider road, with, to our delight, a footpath for quite some time.

It was 5 p.m. when we finally reached the Drovers Inn at Inverarnan. We left our waterproofs in the car and went in to what was already a packed pub for something to eat and drink. I knew that the pub was popular with walkers on the West Highland Way, which followed the east bank of Loch Lomond as opposed to the A82 which took the west bank. Presumably, it was that popularity which meant that all accommodation in Inverarnan, including at the pub itself, was fully booked and why it was already heaving at 5p.m. We managed to get a table and had a couple of drinks and a meal of smoked mackerel, relaxing and enjoying the ambience of what was a really atmospheric old pub before leaving at 6:30 for Inverbeg.

Back at The Corries, I fulfilled my reputation as a midge magnet by getting bitten, the damp weather and wooded, hillside location having drawn out hordes of the little blighters. The Euro 2000 football tournament had just begun, so we watched Holland play the Czech Republic and reflected on what, despite our initial trepidation and the wet weather, had not been too bad a day. Sadly, our reverie was rudely interrupted by the weather forecast for the next day; heavy rain and gale force winds. Ah well, we were in the west of Scotland and at least we were well prepared for it.

Day 41 Monday 12 June 2000 Inverarnan to Tyndrum

We knew that we had, at about 11 miles, a relatively short day in front of us so spent longer than usual talking to fellow guests this morning. The couple from Pemberton that we met yesterday had lived in Shrewsbury, probably our favourite Midlands' town, and in Scotland before emigrating to Australia and were really good company. We then got chatting to another Australian couple, this time from Brisbane. They had just watched, and filmed, a mink kill two rabbits on the land in front of the Guest House. So it was 9:45, late for us, by the time we drove away from the Corries bound for Tyndrum. Before we left, Mrs Carruthers had given us the telephone number for the Kings House Hotel at the end of Rannoch Moor where we would hope to stop on Tuesday night.

It was 11 a.m. before we started walking from the Drovers Arms at Inverarnan. Before we left, I used the phone in the pub to try and book in at the Kings House Hotel but they were fully occupied for the following night. The weather was damp and overcast but the heavy gales and high winds forecast the night before had not yet materialised. It wasn't long before we had an unforeseen encounter that delayed us for twenty minutes or so, however. All traffic, including pedestrians, was held up by a farmer and assorted helpers who were moving a flock of sheep from one field to another via the A82. They were aided and abetted by no less than 6 sheep dogs but the operation was not going smoothly. My experience of sheep control was limited to a popular BBC programme called 'One Man and His Dog', in which a lone shepherd and his faithful border collie would contrive, via a series of whistles from the shepherd and deft positioning by the dog, to manoeuvre half a dozen or so sheep around a series of obstacles. It was all very genteel and invariably greeted with polite applause by the audience. What unfolded in front of us was not so decorous. The sheep were particularly recalcitrant and the dogs were, like all dogs are, descended from wolves.

However, I suspect that in the case of this farmer's dogs, the ancestral lineage was a lot more recent than that for most other dogs. Any sheep foolish enough to try and make a break for it was literally seized upon by at least two of the shepherd's canine enforcers and dragged back into line. I suspect that this would have meant instant disqualification in the aforesaid BBC programme but it made for an illuminating interlude for us. And following my experience with the labrador at Lesmahagow, I made sure that I kept my hands out of my pockets!

Entertainment over, we continued on to Crianlarich, reaching there at 1:15 p.m. after a walk of six miles or so. The railway station tea room was popular with walkers who had taken a small detour from the West Highland Way and, as often before, we lingered over our lunch of cheese toasties and fruit slices with mugs of tea. When we left at 2:30, the heavens had opened, as promised, and we passed a pretty miserable hour and a half amidst heavy traffic before reaching Glengarry House, our overnight halt just short of the centre of Tyndrum. En route, we were able to give directions on how to get back onto the West Highland Way to a couple of walkers who had gone astray. We also spotted a misguided hiker with a particularly full pack wearing only a T-shirt on his upper body. I can only hope he avoided hypothermia.

Jim Mailer, the host at Glengarry, was a really nice guy. He took our waterproofs and shoes to his drying room and offered to do a large bag of our laundry for £4. And although he could not accommodate us on the next night, he volunteered to collect us from the remote Kings House Hotel for £10 as we should be able to find another room in Tyndrum fairly easily. In fact, I booked in at the Inverary Hotel just 200 yards up the road for the following night within minutes. There were just two drawbacks, our room did not have a television and England were playing their first match in Euro 2000 this evening. And then we heard Jim practising the bagpipes.

We left Jim to what should always be a solitary pursuit and drove back to Inverarnan to collect our other car. On the way, we stopped off at the Inverary Hotel to see if they would be showing the England game that night; they would. By 7 p.m., we were back in the Hotel, showered, changed and ready for a meal and to watch the match. We got talking to a Scottish lorry driver and a Dutch couple on holiday, the meal was good and the game kicked off. And then it happened. Paul Scholes scored for England after 3 minutes. I could not contain my delight and celebrated fairly exuberantly and, it soon transpired, fairly solitarily. Not long afterwards, England scored again. Cue more exuberance from me, more disdain from the watching Scots. I tactfully refrained from pointing out that they had not even qualified for the tournament, having been eliminated by England in the play-off round and sat back to enjoy what would surely be a comfortable England win.

It wasn't to be. Just four minutes after the second England goal, Portugal pulled one back. The bar erupted. Fifteen minutes later, Portugal equalised. Same story. And when Portugal scored what proved to be the winning goal in the second half there was pandemonium. Scottish animosity towards England in matters of football was legendary but we were experiencing it directly for the first time and in what was a relatively refined bar. Thank God we weren't in Ecclefechan! Our Dutch companions found the level of antagonism surprising, saying that it just would not happen if their neighbours Belgium were playing. It was a very subdued couple that made their way back to Glengarry House at 11. Sometimes I just hate football...

Day 42 Tuesday 13 June 2000 Tyndrum to Kings House Hotel

We had breakfast at 7:30, knowing that we faced a long and testing day that would include a transit of Rannoch Moor, renowned as a challenging environment and one of the last remaining wildernesses in Europe. Jim Mailer had already done the laundry that we had given him the previous night and confirmed that he would pick us up if we gave him a ring once we got to Kings House. The weather forecast was for heavy rain and strong winds in the morning with a possibility of the rain abating in the afternoon but the high winds continuing. We prepared as best we could by including changes of socks and shoes in our day pack and were confident that our waterproofs would not let us down so set out at 9:15 prepared, we hoped, for whatever lay ahead of us.

As we stocked up on Kit Kats and Kendal Mint Cake in Tyndrum village shop we got chatting to a couple who were walking the West Highland Way. The girl told us that some people had already turned back from Rannoch Moor as the weather was so bad. I could understand that as the Way would doubtless include difficult terrain over the Moor but we decided that as we would be on tarmac we would press on, at least as far as Bridge of Orchy which was some six miles away and had a railway station that would deliver us back to Tyndrum if need be.

Almost as soon as we left the shop the wind, rain and hail kicked in. The road started to incline and we experienced what were certainly the most challenging conditions we had faced so far. Weather like that was particularly trying for spectacle wearers like me, confronted with minimal visibility. In a little while, we came across a car in a lay by. It was the Dutch couple that we had chatted to in the hotel bar whilst watching the football the previous night. They were on their way to Fort William and had kindly stopped to offer us a lift, even though we were soaking wet. Of course, we had to decline but we chatted for a few minutes before they wished us well and left us to tackle the wind and rain.

By 11:30 we had reached the Bridge of Orchy Hotel, wet but unbowed. The Hotel was already hosting a sizeable contingent of walkers taking temporary refuge from the West Highland Way, which crossed the A82 at this point. We had a drink and decided that, as food was served from 12 noon, we had better have lunch there as there would be nowhere else before Kings House Hotel. Over what was a welcoming and decent lunch we talked to a very nice French girl from Caen in Brittany who was doing the Way by herself, replete with large rucksack, during a break from her job as a dietician in Norwich. She had my utmost admiration and we wished her a sincere 'bon chance' as she left, heading like us, for Kings House but via a far more difficult route. We followed her out some ten minutes later at 1 pm, reinvigorated by both our lunch and our encounter with the brave mademoiselle.

Despite the forecast, there was no sign of the rain abating. We had no option but to plough onwards and, more obviously now, upwards. At 2:30 we came to one of the roadside snack bars that had been a frequent feature of Devon and Cornwall but were a rarity in this part of the world. We took advantage of the attached canopy to enjoy fifteen minutes respite from the rain over steaming mugs of tea but all too soon we were underway again. By now, our shoes and socks were absolutely sodden but there would have been no point in changing them; that luxury would have to wait for Kings House.

By 4 pm, the rain finally eased slightly but the high wind continued unabated as at last we breasted the summit of Rannoch Moor, marked with a sign giving the altitude as 1141 ft. The pictures we took there give a good indication of what really was a desolate but magnificent wilderness. Sadly, in retrieving the camera from the rucksack I realised that the driving rain had even penetrated what I had thought was an impermeable lining to it and our spare socks were wet through. Luckily, the spare shoes had escaped, so we would have something dry to wear once we got to Kings House.

The sun finally emerged as we tackled the last three miles or so, able at last to appreciate the splendour of our surroundings as we dried out, feet excepted, in the now relatively warm wind. We passed the Glencoe Ski Centre on our left before finally reaching the Kings House Hotel at 5:20, tired but absolutely elated with ourselves at what we had achieved. We had walked nearly 20 miles in what really were atrocious conditions but both agreed that it had been one of the most exhilarating days of our lives. We had never felt more alive.

By 6:45 we were back at Glengarry Guest House in Tyndrum. We had rung Jim Mailer and, good as his word, he had immediately set out to collect us. While we waited, we changed our soaking socks and shoes for dry shoes and relaxed over a drink. We were sad to say goodbye to Jim, who was a really nice guy, but he had no vacancies that night so we drove the short distance to the Inverary Hotel, scene of last night's football episode. The atmosphere was, of course, nothing like as febrile tonight and we were able to enjoy our dinners, still buzzing at the day's events. I managed to book accommodation for the next three nights and Carol phoned Alison at home to learn that all was well there. And as we watched the local news we learned that Scotland had experienced its deepest depression in thirty years and windiest June on record. As if we needed telling!

Day 43 Wednesday 14 June 2000 Kings House Hotel to Ballachulish

Much as we had enjoyed our wild day yesterday, we were looking forward to a quieter day today. We were only scheduled to do 13 miles or so, one of our shorter daily distances, so took our time over breakfast. Carol opted for what was described as a Scottish breakfast and included porridge, kippers and oatcakes. I stuck with more traditional fare and we were ready to set out from the Inverary Hotel by 9:45.

At 11:10 we were back at the Kings House Hotel, our finishing point last night, having left a car at the Lyn Leven Guest House at Ballachulish. Today was cool and breezy but thankfully dry and we were able to take in more of the dramatic scenery as we ferried our cars. Glencoe in particular looked imposingly grand and we were looking forward to walking the length of it. As we set out, we were walking parallel to the West Highland Way and could see many brightly clad and heavily laden walkers who were, I am sure, as relieved as us to be out of the rain. Traffic was fairly light, which was just as well as there was no footpath in such a remote part of Scotland but it was a simple enough matter to step onto the grass verge as a vehicle approached.

After three miles or so, the West Highland Way took a sharp right, heading uphill and cross country via the ominously named Devil's Staircase on its way to Kinlochleven. We stuck to the easier gradient that the A82 afforded and were treated to a fly past by three RAF jets on a training flight down the Glen. We may not have heard them coming but certainly heard them as they thundered past, flying at what seemed to me to be no more than 200 feet above ground level. There were few signs of habitation in the Glen and I would imagine it would be all but impossible to get planning permission for any building in such a glorious setting. However, we did eventually happen upon a simple white cottage on the right side of the road. We had heard yesterday when chatting to a couple of Scotsmen at the roadside snack bar that the disc jockey Jimmy Savile had a holiday house in Glencoe and this was evidently it. At the time, he was regarded as a flamboyant but good hearted celebrity who had been knighted in 1990 for raising many millions of pounds for charitable causes. Not long after his death in 2009 however it emerged that he was a prolific predatory sex offender and that is how he will inevitably be remembered.

It wasn't long before we came to a designated viewing point and decided to take some pictures of what really was an imposing scene. Sadly, yesterday's weather had done for our camera and try as I might I could not get it to work. We pressed on, eventually arriving at 2:30 at the impressive Glencoe Visitor Centre run by the National Trust for Scotland. Here, we had some lunch and learnt something of the history of the Glen, particularly from a 14 minute video presentation of the Massacre of Glencoe where, in 1692, 38 members of the MacDonald clan had been murdered by Government troops under the command of a Captain Robert Campbell. Another 40 or so died from exposure, having had to flee their homes on a bitterly cold February night. Animosity between the MacDonald and Campbell clans was long standing and apparently, some say, still continues to this day, although I strongly suspect that this is more for the benefit of the tourist trade than in reality.

We left the Visitor Centre after an hour and made our leisurely way to Glencoe village where we had a drink at the Glencoe Hotel. Yesterday's exertions had taken their toll and we were both feeling a little tired so we didn't rush. We were gone by 5:30 and took our time over the final couple of miles alongside Loch Leven, with views forward to the Nevis range, finally reaching our guest house at 6:30. Our final task for the day was to fetch the first car from Kings House. This gave us two more chances to take in the grandeur of Glencoe and I have to say it was the most impressive stretch of the walk to date. Hot baths and a call home to Laura rounded off the day and, seemingly as ever on our walk, we slept really well. I would recommend a day's walk in Glencoe to anyone tired of life or suffering from insomnia; it really is magnificent.

Day 44 Thursday 15 June 2000 Ballachulish to Fort William

The weather forecast for today was good and we were on the road driving to Fort William by 9:15. Twenty five years earlier, we would have had to take to take a fifteen mile diversion around Loch Leven via Kinlochleven to get from South Ballachulish to North Ballachulish and thence on to Fort William but the bridge built in 1975 across Loch Leven at its narrowest point effectively saved us a day. Prior to 1975, there was a ferry boat service across the loch at that point and old film footage shows that it looked pretty much like a floating bridge. However, no amount of persuading at that time would have convinced me that even if we had walked continuously around the ferry as it made the short crossing that this was legitimate; it would have to have been the long way round via Kinlochleven.

Glenlochy Guest House lay just to the north of Fort William and in the lee of Ben Nevis, Britain's highest mountain. We left one car there and drove back to Ballachulish in the other, stopping en route in Fort William. Here, I found disposable cameras on offer at Boots and bought three for the price of two as replacements for our water damaged original one; those should last us to John O'Groats! Meanwhile, Carol made an appointment to have her hair done in the town the following morning. We would only be walking ten miles or so, or for three hours at our usual pace, so would not start out until after lunch.

We were back pounding the A82 by 11:10 a.m. having left a car at Lyn Leven Guest House and after an hour or so crossed the bridge, this time on foot. I say crossed; eventually crossed would be more appropriate. I challenge anybody crossing Ballachulish Bridge on foot not to pause and take in the views that surrounded us. Loch Linnhe was to our left, Loch Leven on our right. Ahead lay the Nevis Range and behind us Glencoe and we made good use of one of our new cameras in trying to capture the scene.

115

At a garage at Onich we stopped for iced coffees which were very refreshing on what was by now a bright and sunny day; so sunny that we needed to apply sun tan lotion. And to think that just 48 hours earlier we had been crossing Rannoch Moor in a gale. British weather has certainly never lacked variety. Two hours and six miles up the road we started thinking about lunch. A sign pointed to a bistro three quarters of a mile up a road on our right. Seductive as it sounded, we opted against the additional mile and a half walking that this would entail, settling instead for a coffee shop that presented itself a little further on the A82. With hindsight, the extra mile and a half would have been the preferable option. I can honestly say that what finally arrived was horrendous. How can you go wrong with a baked potato, cheese and pickle? Our chef/proprietor certainly did. The cheese was reminiscent of plastic, the pickle anaemic at best but the piece de resistance was an enormous mound of coleslaw, so ubiquitous in Scotland that I was beginning to suspect that it was compulsory with meals north of the border. To rub salt in the wound, within a mile of leaving the coffee shop we passed a lovely loch side pub where we could have had a bar meal and refreshing shandy. Such is life…

The next four miles were a little testing; the A82 was quite busy and we had to avoid oncoming traffic by stepping onto what was a very rough road side verge. Thereafter, we had the benefit of a footpath alongside Loch Linnhe and could relax and stride out. Somewhat deceptively, we passed a sign saying 'Fort William' but were a good two miles short of the town centre and getting hungry and thirsty. The hotel we came to at 4:45 promised that it was open to non-residents, however our enquiries revealed that it would not serve drinks before 5! The West End Hotel that we reached at 5 allowed us a shandy but would not serve us food before 6:30. And this in a town that relies almost completely upon tourism. Finally, we got something to eat and drink in the Ossian Bar in the town centre.

We made it to the Glenlochy Guest House by 7 p.m. and watched television for a while to unwind after what I can best describe as a curate's egg of a day, i.e., good in parts. Having fetched our car from Ballachulish, we made our usual round of phone calls and I was able to book accommodation in Fort Augustus on Saturday, ensuring that there was a television in our room. England were playing Germany that night in the Euro 2000 competition. That would be sure to be a difficult match for England. The Germans had been our footballing nemesis so many times since our victory over them in the 1966 World Cup Final. One thing was for sure, we would not be watching the game in a crowded Scottish bar after our experience in Tyndrum!

Day 45 Friday 16 June 2000 Fort William to Stronaba

We spent the morning looking around Fort William, very much a tourist orientated town. I bought some new trousers, resisting the tartan variety, and Carol got herself a new fleece. After a leisurely cup of coffee, Carol went off to her hair appointment and I went to one of the town's pubs. Last night's meal at the Ossian Bar had been OK, so we went back there for lunch. By 3 p.m. we had collected both cars and were on our way to Springburn Farmhouse at Stronaba, our next overnight stop and one of three that we would be making in the Great Glen as we followed the large geological fault that bisects the Scottish Highlands. The Glen is a natural travelling route which is used by waterways, including the Caledonian Canal, the main A82 road, which we would be walking in general, and, at one time, the Invergarry and Fort Augustus Railway. Its strategic importance in controlling various rebellious clans was emphasised by the construction of Fort William at its southern end, Fort Augustus in the middle and Fort George near Inverness.

We finally started walking at 3:55 p.m., our latest start to a day since Land's End. However, this time we didn't have to worry about fading light. It wouldn't get dark for another six hours or so in mid-June in this northern part of Britain. We did have fairly strong sunlight to contend with and, for the second day running, applied sun tan lotion. The A82 headed slightly inland as it made its way towards Spean Bridge, some nine miles away. We were blessed with a footpath for the first half mile or so but then had to take evasive action onto the grass verge as vehicles passed us. The weather conditions meant that we had lovely views of Ben Nevis as we walked but also that we got through a fair amount of water on what was probably the hottest day of our walk to date.

At 6:50, we reached Spean Bridge; not bad going considering the heat and traffic. We stopped for drinks and something to eat at the Spean Bridge Hotel before re-joining the A82 which took a sharp uphill left turn not long afterwards. Soon we came to the very imposing bronze Commando Memorial, erected in 1951 to commemorate the dead of the Second World War British Commando Forces who had trained in the vicinity. The three commandos depicted in the sculpture were looking towards Ben Nevis and there were also good views of Aonoch Moor from the plinth that supports the Memorial. Sites like these always strike me as particularly poignant. My father and grandfather had both had to take part in world wars and I counted myself lucky never to have had to take up arms. Like virtually all Brits, however, I have nothing but the greatest admiration for those that did and still do so on our behalf.

It only took twenty minutes to walk the final mile to the very comfortable Springburn Farmhouse and we were really glad of the showers that we enjoyed before collecting the other car from Fort William. It had been a short but warm afternoon's walk and we were both feeling tired. As usual Carol wrote up her notes in bed. As I re-read them in preparation for writing this, I'm surprised to see that she thinks I look a little slimmer. It just goes to show that even after thirty five years of desk-bound indolence something as simple as regular walking can be greatly beneficial and I was feeling the fittest that I had in years.

Day 46 Saturday 17 June 2000 Stronaba to Fort Augustus

Today would be a twenty miler so we were up and breakfasting by 7:30, determined to be in Fort Augustus early enough so that we could fetch our car from Stronaba and be back in time to watch England play Germany. Over our meal, we talked to a Scottish chap who was well into climbing, particularly recommending to us the Torridon Mountains to the north west of where we were. The range included several Munros, mountains over 3000 feet high, of which there were nearly 300 in Scotland, Ben Nevis naturally being the highest. Much as we enjoyed walking, our preference was for the horizontal version but I could easily see the attraction of any outdoor activity in areas such as Glencoe and Loch Lomond that we had passed through.

We were walking again by 10 a.m., having left a car at the Caitref B & B in Fort Augustus. Our journey there and back had shown that there were very few opportunities for getting something to eat and drink so we stocked up well at a nearby garage as we re-joined the busy A82. The weather was overcast and cooler than yesterday and we were grateful for this. As yesterday, there were no footpaths so we resorted to the grass verge as traffic passed but still made fairly good time, eventually stopping after two hours and six miles at the Letterfinlay Lodge Hotel for coffee. We enjoyed this in the hotel lounge overlooking Loch Lochy, relaxing as we took in the beautiful view. The loch was linked to Loch Oich and Loch Ness by the Caledonian Canal and, just like the Norfolk Broads in England, was used by holidaymakers in cabin cruisers. I had enjoyed several holidays on the Broads in my youth but Loch Lochy was on a far grander scale and far less crowded than Norfolk and I had to confess to envying the holidaymakers we were watching. It was around here that we saw at close hand and photographed our first distinctive red deer, although we had sadly seen no less than four dead ones as we walked on Rannoch Moor and in Glencoe.

Not long after leaving the hotel, the road widened and ran directly alongside the loch, providing us with a wide hard shoulder on which to walk safely and admire the view. We stopped at 1:30 and ate our lunches on a grassy bank but were underway again after fifteen minutes; oh for a bench! We crossed the Caledonian Canal at the northern end of Loch Lochy at a place called Laggan via an impressive swing bridge and proceeded up the northern bank of Loch Oich, soon arriving at an entrance to the Great Glen Cycleway that we'd heard about from Adele at Lockerbie. Here we got chatting to a woman who had just descended from the Cycleway. Somehow she persuaded us that the extra half mile or so to Invergarry that would be involved in taking what was the higher ground that she had used would be preferable to the road because of the views and absence of traffic. It wasn't. The steep ascent, uneven ground and even steeper descent probably added at least half an hour to our day and there were midges! I don't mean to sound ungrateful and doubtless she meant well but thereafter we decided to stick to level ground whenever possible.

At Invergarry we got something to eat, my meal including the Scottish speciality of square sausage in a roll. And as it was self-service I managed to avoid the coleslaw. We were gone by 4:30, travelling another two miles or so along the A82 before deciding to take to the Caledonian Canal towpath at Bridge of Oich. The Phillip's Navigator showed that it was pretty much the same distance as the road and I knew enough about canals to know that they didn't go uphill. We had the canal on our right hand and the River Oich on our left and it was lovely walking, marred only by the aches that we were both experiencing in our feet and legs after a hard day. A handy bench gave us five or ten minutes respite before we pressed on, finally arriving at Caitref at 7 p.m., immediately setting out for Stronaba to collect our car.

By 8, we were back at Caitref, sat in two armchairs that Janet and Paddy Paterson had thoughtfully provided in front of a large screen television watching England play. We'd missed the first fifteen minutes but didn't really care as England kept their hopes of progressing alive by beating Germany 1-0 thanks to an Alan Shearer headed goal. With the benefit of that wonderful thing called hindsight, it would have been nice to have watched it in a Scottish bar but we were happy enough with the win. We booked accommodation for the next two nights at Drumnadrochit and Muir of Ord, where, coincidentally, Mrs Paterson had played golf today. Before we went to bed, Carol had to dress a painful blister, ominously close to the site of the one she had to have treated in Cheshire. It had indeed been a hard day.

Day 47 Sunday 18 June 2000 Fort Augustus to Drumnadrochit

Last night, Carol had spotted a bus stop with a timetable. It showed that there was a daily service from Drumnadrochit to Fort Augustus at 9:15. After Carol had re-dressed her blister, we had an early breakfast that included stewed rhubarb from the Patersons' garden before setting out at 8:30 in both cars for Bridgend House at Drumnadrochit, our next stop. The bus turned up on time and we were back in Fort Augustus at 9:45. My only complaint was the cost; we could have had unlimited bus travel around the West Midlands for a week for the extortionate amount that we were charged. By way of mitigation, the driver said that it would have been the same cost if we had travelled all the way from Inverness to Fort Augustus but that somewhat perverse pricing policy did nothing to soften the blow.

Knowing that we would not have to return for a car that night, we took our time, stopping for a cup of coffee and to stock up on snacks. We also spent some time watching holiday boats negotiating the series of locks that linked Loch Ness to the Caledonian Canal. And despite knowing deep down that there could not conceivably be such a thing as the Loch Ness Monster, I could not resist the occasional inquisitive glance at the vast stretch of water that lay before us. As an indication of its size, it contains more fresh water than all the lakes in England and Wales combined and we would be walking about half of its length today.

We finally got underway at 11 a.m. in what was light rain having donned waterproof jackets in readiness. As usual on the A82, there were no footpaths and we took to the grass verge with increasing frequency as the volume of traffic increased. The rain stopped after half an hour, so we removed our waterproofs, only for it to start again shortly afterwards. This happened three times before we arrived at the Glenmoriston Hotel at Invermoriston and decided to stop for lunch. The marketing genius who invented the ploughman's lunch in the 1950's on behalf of the Cheese Marketing Board has got a lot to answer for. It has spawned innumerable imitators; here it was the Crofter's Platter that I opted for and the Fisherman's Platter that Carol chose. I can't vouch for the authenticity of the various items that we were served, although it stretched credulity to imagine two such busy workmen taking time out of a working day to concoct those eponymous dishes, but they were tasty, albeit expensive, and we took our time, staying there until 3 p.m.

I'm not sure if there were marketing geniuses around in the 1930's, when stories of the Loch Ness Monster, first mooted in the 6th century, re-emerged but the intriguing if unlikely possibility of a surviving dinosaur in the shape of a plesiosaur caught the public imagination and a whole tourist industry sprang up around the loch. And, just as this morning, I could not stop myself from occasionally scanning the loch as we strode out after lunch, anxious to get a move on as we still had thirteen miles to go. I'd like to bet that even the most sceptical of visitors does the same. The sun had emerged by now and we forsook the opportunity to ascend to the Great Glen Cycleway as we came to an entrance; we had learnt our lesson from yesterday. We did however pause to chat to a Forestry Commission worker busy trimming bushes. He knew Adele Beck, our acquaintance from Lockerbie, well and promised to pass on our best wishes as she did not work on Sundays.

We walked briskly for five miles then stopped for a drink. Another hour at the same pace meant that we had broken the back of the thirteen miles so we stopped again and Carol attended to her blister which was giving her quite some grief. As we enjoyed a drink, we heard a screeching of brakes from behind us followed by an almighty bang. Turning back to see if we could help we found that a van driver had misjudged a bend and collided with the rock face on his left. He was fine but the van had suffered significant damage. He had his own mobile phone, still something of a rarity at that time, so was able to summon help and we left him to it. It was now quite warm, although nowhere near as hot as the Midlands of England where temperatures, we later learnt, had been in the 80's Fahrenheit. We had to press on and eventually passed a stone commemorating the racing driver John Cobb who had lost his life at that point on Loch Ness at a speed of over 200 miles per hour whilst attempting to break the world water speed record. Not long afterwards, we came to Urquhart Castle on our right and knew that we only had a mile and a half to go. After half that distance, we stopped at Lewiston for a drink and a rest, both by now feeling the effects of two relatively long consecutive days walking. It was two very weary travellers that finally arrived at the pretty village of Drumnadrochit and we were grateful not to have to fetch a car as we turned in for an early night.

Day 48 Monday 19 June 2000 Drumnadrochit to Muir of Ord

It was now time to leave the A82, which had been pretty much our constant companion since Glasgow and would continue on to Inverness, and head inland towards Beauly and Dingwall. We had been woken in the night by a thunderstorm but this had cleared the air and it was a warm day with a nice breeze by the time we set out to drive to Muir of Ord at 9:30. By 10:50 we were walking, having again stocked up on snacks and drinks at the village shop knowing that the first part of our day would afford few opportunities to do so. Our final act before leaving was to leave a parking permit that the chatty landlady Roz has given to us in our car, which would be parked on the village green all day.

After a mile or so on the A831 we took a right turn on to the A833, more or less immediately beginning what would be two miles of steep ascent, initially one in seven for three quarters of a mile then one in six for a mile and a quarter. All but the hardiest of cyclists had dismounted and joined us in walking and we were grateful for the grassy bank where we sat and enjoyed a drink as we reached the summit of the climb. The next stretch was pretty uneventful. We were walking across moorland dotted with those two archetypal Scottish perennials, gorse and heather, and there were good views back to Drumnadrochit but other than that it was a question of just ticking off the miles as we made progress northwards.

At 2 p.m. we reached the Brockies Lodge Hotel at Kiltarlity, getting our timing right for once as food would be served until 2:30. We stopped for an hour and a half, enjoying lasagne and chicken curry and talking to the proprietor, the only Scotsman I'd ever met with a Sean Connery accent, and an American cyclist doing an end-to-end trip, with diversions around Wales and the Lake District thrown in for good measure. He was one of a group

126

making the trip and averaging 60-80 miles a day. However, they all rode at their own pace and met up at night at their agreed destination.

As we left the hotel, we reckoned that we had approximately seven miles to go, or just over two hours. We re-joined the A833 for two miles then took a right on to the A862 sign posted for Beauly and for the first time in quite a while took to the footpath! We reached the town at 4:45 and stopped for fifteen minutes for a cup of tea. Carol rang Laura, who had returned to Swansea University for a summer ball, only to learn that she had had her purse and camera stolen as she danced. We did have better fortune in a Beauly store, however, finding that they stocked a particular make of blister plasters that incorporated a blue gel and that had been most effective in treating our multitudinous specimens of that curse of the walker. Even though the troublesome blister on Carol's left heel had eased somewhat, we took the opportunity of stocking up on the product, knowing that we still had another hundred and twenty miles to go and would in all probability need them before we reached John O'Groats.

It was about three miles to our B & B at Muir of Ord along the A862 and we passed its eponymous golf club on our left, remembering as we did Mrs Paterson from Fort Augustus who had played there two days ago. We arrived at 6:15 to find that as we were the only guests we had the T V lounge to ourselves, except for the owner's inquisitive dog, and relaxed for a while before fetching our car from Drumnadrochit. That night, we booked in at the Novar Arms at Evanton for two nights, planning to use that as our base in an area where there would not be much in the way of accommodation. And our expectation was that we would be able to watch England's triumph in its final Euro 2000 group game against Romania in relative comfort as it unfolded on the following night.

Day 49 Tuesday 20 June 2000 Muir of Ord to Evanton.

We decided on a short day today, having averaged nearly 19 miles a day for the last three days. The 770 miles that we had already walked were beginning to take their toll and for the first time we were both really looking forward to finishing our walk. At 8:30, we left for Evanton, driving a slightly longer but quicker for cars route via the A9 than the one we would be walking via the A862. And then we saw it; our first road sign pointing to John O'Groats! This gave our flagging spirits quite a boost and by the time we were back at Muir of Ord and walking again we felt re-energised and ready for the day ahead.

It took just under two hours to walk the six miles to Dingwall via the A862, crossing en route the wide River Conon as it made its way to Cromarty Firth. Fishermen were vigorously casting, presumably for salmon in this part of the world, and it made for an agreeable scene although I'd bet that they had paid a lot of money for the privilege. At Dingwall we had coffee and cake in a café in the pedestrianised town centre before setting off again at noon on the Evanton Old Road, a quiet road that ran parallel to the newer and far busier A862. As we climbed out of Dingwall, we passed a sign pointing to somewhere called Bottacks, which sounded to us more like a mild expletive than a place name. We were rewarded for our climb by views out over Cromarty Firth, including several oil rigs queueing for repair at the Invergordon Oil Rig Base.

By 2:15 we had reached the Novar Arms at Evanton, our earliest ever finish to a day. Despite the short mileage, my back was killing me. Carol too had problems with her feet and we were glad of the short day. We drove back to Muir of Ord and collected our car, stopping in the town for lunch before heading back to Evanton. Here, we started our planning for the next few days and Carol came up with a brainwave. In preparation for the walk, I had assiduously highlighted Noel Blackham's route on our Navigator Atlas, trusting that now, as so far to date, he had opted for the shortest viable way between two points. Noel's way as he headed south had been via Bonar Bridge, quite a way inland, but Carol spotted that a bridge near Tain that carried the A9 over the Dornoch Firth seemed to offer a far shorter option to reach the North Sea. We set out on a recce in one of the cars and sure enough Carol was right. The Dornoch Bridge had not been built when Noel made his trip and by using the route that Carol had spotted we would save nine miles, enabling us to get from Evanton to Golspie on the North Sea coast in two days of about seventeen miles each, easily within our range.

We got back to the Novar Arms in plenty of time for the England v Romania match but before we settled down I booked us in at the Golf Links Hotel at Golspie in two days' time. We would walk as far as Edderton tomorrow, having left a car there first thing in the morning in preparation for the evening trip back to Evanton. On the following day, we would take both cars to Golspie, leave one there, drive back to Edderton, walk to Golspie and collect the car from Edderton on the night. Problem solved, nine miles of walking saved and our path to John O'Groats clear. Well done Carol!

Of course, our run couldn't last. England only needed a point against Romania to qualify for the quarter-finals of Euro 2000. They were drawing 2-2 with just minutes to go when Romania were awarded a penalty. I'd like to say that it was a dodgy one; it wasn't. We were well beaten and our only consolation was to have watched it in our room rather than in the hotel bar. I don't think that I could have taken another 3-2 English loss in a Scottish bar after Tyndrum. As we settled down for the night, I noticed from the paper that the man walking backwards to John O'Groats was now ahead of us despite having set out from Land's End after us. We hadn't seen him pass us and I would have been miffed had he found a short cut but we'll never know

Day 50 Wednesday 21 June 2000 Evanton to Edderton

Our recce yesterday had shown that today's walk would be taking us through a pretty remote part of the country so we stocked up at the local Allday's store in Evanton in readiness. Earlier, we had enjoyed full breakfasts in the Novar Arms, including porridge for Carol which she described as delicious. We had then driven to Edderton, leaving a car in the car park of the Church of Scotland there. It was a Wednesday and our reasoning was that the church would be having a day off; I hope they forgave us our trespasses.

We were walking by 10:30, soon crossing another premium salmon fishing water, the River Glass. We took the B9176 road after about two miles, pausing as we did to take in the view of the now nearby Invergordon Oil Rig base. For two days in 1931, ships of the Royal Navy at Invergordon, then a naval base, were in open mutiny in one of the few military strikes in British history. Experienced ratings were infuriated by what they understood would be a 25% cut in their pay. Their action caused panic on the stock exchange and a run on the pound. Of course, all was now tranquil as we carried on our way. I decided to put on waterproof trousers in what was now steady light rain but Carol decided that the rain would soon pass. She was wrong and before long her trousers were wet through and it was too late for the waterproofs.

We continued on the B9176 in light traffic, initially uphill then down, crossing the Alness River as it made its way to Cromarty Firth. At 12:30 we paused for lunch, using the steps of the abandoned Castle Inn for undercover seating. After 20 minutes we were walking again. The sun had finally appeared and I took my waterproofs off before we passed Ardross, marked by a small school and a scattering of houses. We then passed through Ardross Forest, with trees on both sides of us as we did so. We eventually emerged into open moorland, covered with gorse and heather, which seemed to go on for an eternity.

At 2 p.m., we sat on a handy low wall for drinks and a rest. Carol's trousers had dried out now in the sun, helped by a pleasant breeze but soon the skies darkened significantly. We were prepared this time and both had waterproofs on before the heavens opened, treating us to hailstones in addition to heavy rain. A thick mist then descended and we had to take great care, thankful that there was not a lot of traffic on this particular stretch of road. Suddenly, the Aultnamain Inn loomed out of the mist; what would we not give for something warm to drink in front of a roaring log fire? It was closed, of course, and up for sale and we had no alternative but to press on. A generous soul driving a Range Rover stopped and offered us a lift, out of the question, of course, but his kindness was much appreciated and we explained what we were doing and why we had to decline. He probably thought us mad to be out on such an afternoon.

After half a mile, the first leg of Carol's short cut came into play. On our right, an unmarked, single track road with passing places would lead us four miles or so to Edderton. We decided to get a move on; our feet were soaking and we wanted to finish as quickly as we could. At 3:45 the rain finally stopped and the mist disappeared. Our spirits were sufficiently lifted that I got the camera out and took a picture of Carol in splendid isolation in the middle of nowhere and absolutely surrounded by gorse in full flower; it's one of my favourite photos of the whole trip. As we eventually descended into Edderton at 4:20 we were treated to a sight of the second leg of Carol's short cut, the impressive bridge over Dornoch Firth. And, bless them, the Church of Scotland elders had not clamped our car. We would not have got away with that in Birmingham.

It was bliss to get back to the warm and comfortable Novar Arms Hotel. Hot showers soon made up for the weather we had experienced, probably second only in its severity to our day on Rannoch Moor. For once, we did not have to fetch a car and were able to enjoy a lovely meal and a few drinks at our leisure. Back in our room, I booked us accommodation at Helmsdale and Latheronwheel on the forthcoming Saturday and Sunday. It struck me as I did so that all that would then be remaining would be to book in at Wick in readiness for the last leg. We were getting there!

Day 51 Thursday 22 June 2000 Edderton to Golspie

Anybody who knows Carol will acknowledge how intelligent she is. She has lived in Britain all her life and knows, as we all do, that the British weather is variable at best. Yesterday, she got soaked as we walked, through not putting her waterproof trousers on in time. Today, she decided not to take them with her at all. I can do no better than reproduce the note that she made in her diary on the evening: 'BIG MISTAKE'.

As usual, we had paid full attention to the weather forecast in the morning before setting out and were promised the occasional shower. It was a bright, warm and humid day as we started walking at 10:30 from the deserted car park at the Church of Scotland, having left our first car at our hotel for the night at Golspie before driving to Edderton in our second car. The first three miles were uneventful and we joined the A9 after an hour, soon starting the crossing of what was then one of the longest bridges in Europe. It started raining almost immediately, so I put on my waterproof trousers. It didn't take long to work out that this was more than an occasional shower and, for the second day running, poor Carol got completely soaked as it poured down. There was absolutely no prospect of sheltering. All we could do was press on at top speed, stopping after four miles at a garage for a little bit of respite and to buy chocolate bars. En route, we had passed on our left Skibo Castle, already scene of several celebrity weddings and later that year to host the wedding of the singer Madonna to the film director Guy Ritchie. We were too pre-occupied to do anything but cast a cursory glance in its direction, however.

Some two miles further on from the garage we came to the Trentham Hotel at a place called Poles. We had spotted this as we drove back from Golspie to Edderton and thankfully it was open. We ordered lunch and while we waited a bedraggled Carol disappeared to the ladies for what seemed an eternity. When she returned, she confessed that she had tried to use the electric hand drier to dry her trousers. I thought of asking her to demonstrate the contortions that this had involved but then thought better of it. In any event, I had my own tribulations to contend with as my feet were soaking.

We were gone from the pub at 2:45. It was still raining but nowhere near as heavily and after an hour or so we passed on our left the road leading to Bonar Bridge, Noel's chosen route. At 4 p.m. we crossed a bridge over Loch Fleet and saw a road sign indicating that it was four miles to Golspie, something of a godsend as we thought that it was five miles. Every mile counts when you are tired, wet and dispirited. Traffic was moving quickly and soon we came across the police dealing with the aftermath of a crash between a car and a lorry on the A9. At 5:15 we reached Golspie and the North Sea, an absolute landmark for us. The small town was dominated by a 100ft statue of the Duke of Sutherland atop Ben Bhraggie. His Grace, or whatever the mode of address might be, had earned deserved notoriety for himself in the early nineteenth century for his part in the Highland Clearances. Apparently, it would be more profitable for the estate to turn the land over to large scale sheep farming, and so the tenants would have to go, whether they wanted to or not. So much for 'noblesse oblige' and I wondered how many displaced crofters had contributed by subscribing to the fund that had paid for the erection of the statue. Less than one, I'd have thought.

Carol was in the bath by 5:30 in the Golf Links Hotel, our home for the night. Refreshed and in dry clothes and shoes at last we set out for Edderton at 6:30, passing another car crash on the A9 as we did so. We would need to be careful tomorrow as we spent the day on that busy road but had already learnt a valuable lesson from today. Almost invariably, we walked facing oncoming traffic. However, on occasions it was what was approaching from behind that was the danger. The temptation was to relax if nothing was coming towards us but traffic travelling in the same direction as us would use that opportunity to overtake, passing perilously close to us as it did so. Oh for some rear view mirrors…

The round trip to Edderton did not take too long and we had a snack in the hotel restaurant. Our last acts before turning in were for me to ring my brother Philip. In all probability, he would fly up from London for the final day's walk, meeting us in Wick. We also rang our friends Braidwood and Jim, arranging to meet them for a meal in Glasgow as we made an overnight stop there on the way home. Finally, we checked on the forecast for tomorrow, colder with yet more rain. We were brassed off with Scottich rain by now but vowed that it would be full waterproofs and extra layers tomorrow. Nothing was going to stop us now.

Day 52 Friday 23 June 2000 Golspie to Helmsdale

Did Carol forget her vow and repeat her 'big mistake' of yesterday? Of course not! Our day sack was relatively full and we were wearing extra layers as we set out from Golspie at 10:30, although the weight of the sack was nothing like that which we had first carried from Land's End. As per usual, we had first left a car at our destination for the night Helmsdale. We would be walking the A9 all day and passed a town called Brora on our way to Helmsdale in the cars. It was seven miles north of Golspie and seemed the ideal spot for lunch, mainly because it was the only real opportunity on the route! Thereafter, it would be ten miles of us against the elements and the forecast had been cloudy with blustery winds and showers. I wonder how far you would have to drive from Birmingham or London before there was a ten mile gap between meal opportunities? Many a mile, I'm sure.

We stocked up on snacks in Golspie and after a mile passed the entrance to Dunrobin Castle, the ancestral stately home of the Earls and Dukes of Sutherland, including, of course, the one immortalised on top of Ben Bhraggie. The fairytale castle looked like something that would not be out of place in Disneyland, complete with turrets and spires, but we had other things on our mind and resisted the opportunity to add to the present incumbent's coffers by taking a tour.

We were in Brora for 12:30 having lunch in a café. I had fish and chips with, you'll never guess what, coleslaw! Never before or since have I seen that combination but it seems a compulsory addition to meals in some Scottish eating establishments. In fairness, the owner did recommend that for puddings we had one of the world famous Capaldi ice creams from the nearby shop and they were very nice. There's a picture of Carol eating hers in front of the clock

136

at Brora in our album of the trip. I'm glad she enjoyed it because now we really had a stint in front of us.

The weather as we set out again at 2 p.m. on what was just a day or two after the summer solstice now seemed unseasonably cold to me, far chillier than the morning had been. It was very windy and we were mightily glad of the extra layers as we walked into the headwind. For a while, we had the railway line for company, separating us from what was a surprisingly blue North Sea, although I bet it was freezing cold, and some lovely, albeit deserted, sandy beaches. We then headed slightly inland, passing through the hamlets of Lothbeg and Lothmore before the final lonely five mile stretch to Helmsdale. We didn't even have much traffic for company and were too wind buffeted to appreciate fully the scenery, far grander than anything in the Midlands. Carol's legs were aching quite a bit and as we sat on a wall for a rest we agreed that we had just about enough left in us for the final three days. Roll on John O'Groats!

We finally crossed a bridge over the River Helmsdale and into the town at 6 p.m. The place seemed deserted but the Belgrave Arms was open and we stopped for a drink and a snack, and as much as anything for a rest, before reaching our B&B at Navidale, just north of the town, at 7 p.m. Again, we were blessed with a lovely hostess and Mrs Polson made us tea and biscuits. We spent some time chatting to her and another Australian couple, this time from Brisbane. They had spotted us near Dunrobin Castle and Mrs Polson had seen us twice on the road during the day.

At 8, we went to collect the other car. Back in our room, I made the final accommodation booking for two nights in Wick. I then rang Philip and he confirmed that he would join us in Wick and walk the final leg, so I managed to get him a room in the same place as us. Finally, I revisited my coping strategy of expressing what remained of a task in percentage terms; 835 miles done, 51 to go, just under 6%. I should be able to sleep easy, and did.

Day 53 Saturday 24 June 2000 Helmsdale to Latheronwheel

Today we would be leaving scenic and hilly Sutherland and entering Caithness, the largely flat county that would provide the background to the last two days of our walk. We still had some climbing to do before then and our early morning recce as we ferried a car to Latheronwheel showed several stiff passages, not much in the way of habitation and few comfort halts. A big breakfast was definitely on the menu and we both had the whole works, porridge plus the full Scottish. Over breakfast, the couple from Brisbane explained that they were researching the wife's family tree, her mother's maiden name being Sutherland. I'm not sure if she was related to the Dukes thereof, but he was definitely Australian aristocracy, being a fifth generation descendant of a convict transported in the 1840's.

We set out on the A9 at 10:15, twisting and turning as we ascended what I think is known as the Ord of Caithness, dominating the coastline at this point. Our Brisbane friends passed us on this stretch, giving us a pip and a cheery wave as they made their way to John O'Groats. We then levelled out for quite a time, eventually coming upon the deserted clearance village of Bad Bea some two hours after leaving Helmsdale. Although we didn't descend down to the village, part way down a steep cliff, it was clearly a remote and desolate spot. In 1840, twelve families set up home here, having been evicted to make way for sheep by one of the landed gentry. I could certainly empathise, my Irish relatives had told me a little of our family history which included two Cremin brothers having to walk many a mile from the far South West of Ireland in the potato famine years of the 1840's to where they eventually settled in County Cork. Their descendants included my father.

We sat on a convenient concrete slab just after Bad Bea and had our emergency supplies; drinks and Kit-Kats. It wasn't the weather to linger, however, far too cold, and we were off again after ten minutes or so. Not long afterwards, we began the nearly mile long steep descent into Berriedale, stopping at the post office there to post cards and give Alison a ring at home. Of course, where there's a steep descent there's usually a steep ascent and so it proved at Berriedale. In fact, so impractical and costly was the crossing of what is known as the Berriedale Braes it meant that the rail line from Inverness to Wick had to be diverted inland rather than follow the east coast of Caithness.

Our next landmark was Dunbeath Castle, situated on a rocky peninsula and steeped in history but now in private ownership. Just afterwards, and thirteen miles into the day, we finally found a shop advertising tea, coffee and hot snacks for sale so went in, as much as anything to get out of the cold. The kindly owner made us cups of tea and provided fold up garden chairs for us to sit in. Carol signed her visitors' book, perhaps a sign that passing trade was scant at best, and noticed that the man walking backwards to John O'Groats had beaten us to it by four days. I wonder how he managed the Berriedale Braes? With care and slowly, I'd have thought. The proprietress also told us that she had cooked for the then Queen Mother at Dunbeath Castle once, easily trumping my own Queen Mother story which I'm including because it's been such a quiet day on the road and we are nearing the end. I was walking past Birmingham Council House in the 1990's one day when a limousine drew up outside and out stepped the diminutive royal personage. For once, there were no welcoming crowds and looking around her glance fell upon me. I was bestowed with a regal wave and smile and, arch republican though I am, good manners dictated that I grudgingly smile back. Perhaps due deference is a genetic trait in us all?

We carried on into Dunbeath but there was nothing to detain us there. On our way out, however, we stopped at the tea rooms attached to the Crofters'

Museum and had soup, rolls, tea and cake. Lovely! The last two miles to our B&B were a battle against the wind and we finally got there at 6 p.m. Betty and Sandy Kennedy were a really lovely couple and made us cups of tea before we went back to Helmsdale for something to eat at the Bannockburn Inn there and to collect our car. Back at the Kennedys we sat in their lounge taking in the view from their picture window; it would still be light for hours yet. Betty told us that she had seen us approaching from a mile away. We also took in one of the Euro 2000 quarter finals but as England had ceased to feature I could not summon up any enthusiasm and it wasn't long before we turned in for the night.

Day 54 Sunday 25 June 2000 Latheronwheel to Wick

It's easy to get spoilt in Scotland, particularly for city dwellers like Carol and I. Yes, it had more than its fair share of rain, the midges were a nuisance and not everybody wants coleslaw with every meal. But I challenge anybody with a soul to walk the length of it, as we had virtually done, and not fall in love with places like Loch Lomond, the hills around Moffat, Glencoe, Ballachulish, the Great Glen and Sutherland. I could go on. There's higher mountains and deeper valleys elsewhere, for sure, but the glorious combination of lochs, just-the-right-height mountains, gorse and heather and the ever-changing shades of light would surely take some beating anywhere in the world. We both agreed that the Scottish leg of our trip had been far and away the highlight of our walk but as if to test us just one more time we would be denied such scenic delights today in Caithness. It would be a case of getting to Wick, our final overnight stop, another seventeen miles under our belts and just another seventeen to go to journey's end.

We had left a car at the White Gables B&B in Wick, stopping off in the town to stock up on emergency rations as once again we would be pretty much in splendid isolation for most of the day. It was 11 a.m. before we started walking; we had stopped to talk to Betty and Sandy at Latheronwheel. Although it was cold, there was no rain and we set out at a good pace. The A9, and most of the traffic, headed off to our left towards Thurso after a mile and we had the A99 pretty much to ourselves. After four miles we stopped at the Portland Arms at Lybster for a cup of coffee and to read the papers. Sunday lunch was being prepared and looked and smelled lovely but we had enjoyed big breakfasts and it was too early for us. We did linger for an hour, though, and it almost seemed that we were demob happy already. This would never do and we started out again, determined to get a move on.

Nothing much happened for the next nine miles or so, other than we kept walking. There were isolated houses dotted along the road and the occasional farm but little traffic. Two 'low-level' cyclists, i.e. those that recline on their backs with the pedals at the front of the bike, passed us, presumably doing an end-to-end run. In reality, the last thirty five miles, or first thirty five if you are heading south, to John O'Groats would make an ideal finish or start for a cyclist, not too taxing and the chance to wind down or get some mileage into the legs. A car then stopped and our landlady from Wick told us that she was going out but had left a note for Philip who would be arriving there that afternoon. We eventually reached the Old Smiddy Inn at Thurmster, four miles short of Wick and, as you do, went in for a drink. As we relaxed, a familiar looking figure went past; Philip had walked out from Wick and joined us for a 'livener'. It was good to see him and we were glad of his company as we finished the last four mile stint to Wick, reaching there at 6:15.

As we walked, Phil described how he had arrived at Wick at 2:30 and straightaway gone into the wrong house, settling down to watch the Euro 2000 competition in a stranger's armchair, doubtless commentating in the process. That would have been very much par for the course for Phil; eccentric, restless, always on the go and with plenty to say. He had a big, big heart though and died far too early aged 57 in 2009. I miss him dearly.

Whilst Carol had a shower, Phil came with me to Latheronwheel to drive our second car back to Wick. We all then adjourned to the Queens Hotel for what was the best meal that we'd had for some time. Back at White Gables I booked a room for Carol and me in Glasgow on Tuesday night and finally asked for breakfast at 7:30 tomorrow morning. We wanted to make an early start as we had a big day ahead of us.

143

Day 55 Monday 26 June 2000 Wick to John O'Groats

This was it, our last day on the road. We had set out into very much the unknown exactly two months ago, walked on 55 of those days, averaging just over sixteen miles a day, and were about to achieve what we had talked about for so long, walk the length of our country. We had breakfast at 7:30 and Carol, Philip and I were on our way by 8:30. There was no need to shuttle a car. Braidwood had kindly supplied me with a bus timetable from John O'Groats; if we missed the bus we would get a taxi back to Wick. A fine day was forecast but we packed our waterproofs, if we had learned anything it was not to trust the British weather. All that remained was to stock up on drinks and chocolate as we passed through the centre of Wick and we were off.

After an hour or so, we passed through Reiss where the A99 turned right and headed due north. Our first rest was after two hours. We sat on the side of the road for a drink and a bite to eat, taking in the wide sweep of Sinclair's Bay as we did so. There were curlews and lapwings galore; birds that you simply would not see in Birmingham. By 11:30 we had made it to Keiss and had a drink and a sandwich at the Sinclair Bay Hotel. A kind soul offered to buy us all a drink. He was spectacularly drunk and I can only assume that this was a continuation from the Saturday night; nobody gets drunk by 11:30 on a Sunday morning, do they? Anyway, we declined his kind offer and got going again by 12 o'clock.

By my calculation, we were now down to single figures in terms of mileage. Nybster came and went, then Freswick, where we rested briefly whilst I rang Jim to finalise arrangements for our meal in Glasgow on Tuesday night. A Yorkshire man a long way from home and working on the garden of his bungalow eventually told us that we had about three miles to go and should be able to see our destination when we crested the next small hill. We came to a sign saying 'John O'Groats 3' had our picture taken, crested the hill and there it was, off to our right! I hadn't realised how close the Orkney Islands were to the mainland and they provided a picturesque backdrop but they could wait for another day; we only had one thing in mind, to finally finish what we had started two months ago.

It took us an hour to do the last stretch which seemed to go on for ever. By now, Carol and I were running completely on empty. All we wanted to do was finish. We came to the village of John O'Groats but had another three quarters of a mile to go. Near to the harbour we had our picture taken beneath a sign pointing to Lands End, 874 miles away. Our last act was to cross, together of course, the white line outside the Groats Inn marking the official end of the journey at 3:30 p.m.; we had made it.

We had just under three hours to kill before our bus back to Wick. Carol bought and wrote forty postcards before somehow summoning up the strength to walk back to the town to post them, thereby ensuring they were postmarked John O'Groats. I could not have walked another fifty yards. We had our 'official' form signed as evidence of our achievement, not that we needed it. We knew what we had done. We chatted to a lovely couple who had cycled the route in three weeks in memory of their daughter, sadly killed by cancer the year before and I was happy to add a tenner to their sponsorship fund. And we finally got to catch up with and talk to a woman who we had seen regularly over the last few days with a very full pack as we ferried our cars. She had done the walk mainly on her own via footpaths, including the high Lairig Ghru pass in the Cairngorms, her husband joining her at weekends when he could. Like us, those people had their intensely personal reasons for making the trip and were rightly celebrating reaching their goal.

145

All that was left for us was to catch the 6:15 bus back to Wick. Carol, Philip and I had the bus to ourselves and I think that it was only then the euphoria really kicked in. Of course we were pleased with ourselves. We had overcome every challenge presented to us. We had beaten the dreaded blisters, midges and coleslaw. Bad weather hadn't stopped us, nor the traffic on Britain's busy roads. Above all, we didn't have to come up with any excuses; we had found our way.

Epilogue

On the Tuesday after we finished, we dropped Phil off at Culloden Battlefield site; he wanted to look around before making his way to Inverness Airport for his flight back to London. I've already mentioned his untimely death but if you want to know the measure of him, there were literally hundreds at his funeral, including the Mayor of Lambeth who re-presented his civic award to me in recognition of all that he had done for Brixton, where he lived and practised law for thirty years. He was a champion of the underdog and afraid of no-one. We drove on to Glasgow for an overnight stop preceded by a meal with Braidwood and Jim, good friends who had been ideal companions on one of our French walking holidays. Jim sadly died recently and we have many fond memories of a true Scottish gentleman.

We were back home in Sutton Coldfield on the Wednesday and reality kicked in. Alison had done a great job in holding the fort but the grass needed cutting, as did the privet. Laura was safely delivered to Gatwick, we both had jobs to go back to, or prepare for; soon it was almost as if we had never been away.

But of course it wasn't. I can honestly say that we had the absolute time of our lives. And it wasn't just memories that the walk gave us; it enriched and empowered us in many ways. It gave us ideas for future holidays, including re-visiting many of the places we had passed through. We tackled the West Highland Way the following year, both even getting proper walking boots for the first time. No big packs, though! There are companies who will book your accommodation and transport your luggage to your next destination each morning, leaving you free to enjoy the day; our kind of walking!

Even now, sixteen years after we finished, we often talk fondly of what we did and plan more trips to stretches we enjoyed. Various ailments mean that I can't walk for more than a mile or two but Carol is as young minded as ever and it's a rare day that she doesn't fit in an hour or so walking. She has even mentioned doing the reverse trip as a solo walker with me as a support driver, something I'd gladly do. But that would mean not seeing our two beautiful grandchildren, Scarlett and Teddy for longer than she could stand. Perhaps when you are 80, Carol?

And it's with Scarlett and Teddy that I'll close. I said on page one of this book that we did the walk for our own satisfaction, which we did. But if it in some small way it inspires them or any future generations to find their own way then Carol and I could not leave a better legacy.

FC

June 2016

Daily destinations and distances

Date	Day	From	To	Miles	Total
26/04/2000	1	Land's End TR19 7AA	Penzance	10.58	10.58
27/04/2000	2	Penzance TR18 2HQ	Pool	15.87	26.45
28/04/2000	3	Pool TR15 3NH	Fraddon	18.87	45.32
29/04/2000	4	Fraddon TR9 6NA	Bodmin	15.25	60.57
30/04/2000	5	Bodmin PL31 2DY	Kennards House	18.34	78.91
01/05/2000	6	Kennards House PL15 8QE	Bridestow	19.89	98.80
02/05/2000	7	Bridestowe EX20 4HZ	Okehampton	6.31	105.11
03/05/2000	8	Okehampton EX20 1EA	Crediton	18.50	123.61
04/05/2000	9	Crediton EX17 1EG	Sampford Peverell	19.55	143.16
05/05/2000	10	Sampford Peverell EX16 7BJ	Taunton	14.50	157.66
06/05/2000	11	Taunton TA1 5NF	Highbridge	19.25	176.91
07/05/2000	12	Highbridge TA9 3AQ	Felton	18.66	195.57
13/05/2000	13	Felton BS48 3DY	Alveston	21.03	216.60
14/05/2000	14	Alveston BS35 3RF	Quedgeley	21.10	237.60
15/05/2000	15	Quedgeley GL2 4RQ	Tewkesbury	12.30	249.90
16/05/2000	16	Tewkesbury GL20 7DB	Kempsey	13.70	263.60
17/05/2000	17	Kempsey WR5 3NB	Kidderminster	21.40	285.00

18/05/2000	18	Kidderminster DY10 1QZ	Wolverhampton	16.80	301.80
19/05/2000	19	Wolverhampton WV1 3AA	Stafford	16.70	318.50
21/05/2000	20	Stafford ST16 2AA	Newcastle-u-Lyme	17.00	335.50
22/05/2000	21	Newcastle-u-Lyme ST5 9EG	Middlewich	18.50	354.00
23/05/2000	22	Middlewich CW10 0JE	Northwich	7.50	361.50
24/05/2000	23	Northwich CW8 4DE	Lowton	17.50	379.00
25/05/2000	24	Lowton WA3 1HE	Charnock Richard	14.30	393.30
26/05/2000	25	Charnock Richard PR7 5LH	Bilsborrow	20.10	413.40
27/05/2000	26	Bilsborrow PR3 0RE	Lancaster	14.80	428.20
28/05/2000	27	Lancaster LA1 1HP	Crooklands	15.20	443.40
29/05/2000	28	Crooklands LA7 7NW	Kendal	7.11	450.51
30/05/2000	29	Kendal LA9 6ES	Shap	15.40	465.91
31/05/2000	30	Shap CA10 3NY	Penrith	12.60	478.51
01/06/2000	31	Penrith CA11 7PX	Carlisle	17.50	494.01
03/06/2000	32	Carlisle CA1 2EL	Gretna Green	10.60	504.61
04/06/2000	33	Gretna Green DG16 5DY	Lockerbie	15.20	519.81
05/06/2000	34	Lockerbie DG11 2DG	Moffatt	17.00	536.81
06/06/2000	35	Moffatt DG10 9QJ	Abington	20.40	557.21
07/06/2000	36	Abington	Lesmahagow	16.00	573.21

		ML12 6TL			
08/06/2000	37	Lesmahagow ML11 0HX	Dalmarnock	23.30	596.51
09/06/2000	38	Dalmarnock G40 4HQ	Dumbarton	16.50	613.01
10/06/2000	39	Dumbarton G82 2QL	Inverbeg	16.40	629.41
11/06/2000	40	Inverbeg G83 8PD	Inverarnan	14.80	644.21
12/06/2000	41	Inverarnan G83 7DX	Tyndrum	11.10	655.31
13/06/2000	42	Tyndrum FK20 8RY	Kings House Hotel	19.20	674.51
14/06/2000	43	Kings House Hotel PH49 4HY	Ballachulish	13.20	687.71
15/06/2000	44	Ballachulish PH49 4JP	Fort William	15.30	703.01
16/06/2000	45	Fort William PH33 6LP	Stronaba	10.60	713.61
17/06/2000	46	Stronaba PH34 4DX	Fort Augustus	20.70	734.31
18/06/2000	47	Fort Augustus PH32 4AY	Drumnadrochit	18.90	753.21
19/06/2000	48	Drumnadrochit IV63 6TX	Muir of Ord	16.20	769.41
20/06/2000	49	Muir of Ord IV6 7XR	Evanton	12.40	781.81
21/06/2000	50	Evanton IV16 9UN	Edderton	15.90	797.71
22/06/2000	51	Edderton IV19 1LF	Golspie	17.40	815.11
23/06/2000	52	Golspie KW10 6TT	Helmsdale	17.70	832.81
24/06/2000	53	Helmsdale	Latheronwheel	16.80	849.61

151

		KW8 6JS			
25/06/2000	54	Latheronwheel KW5 6DS	Wick	17.20	866.81
26/06/2000	55	Wick KW1 5NH	John O'Groats	17.00	883.81

Printed in Great Britain
by Amazon